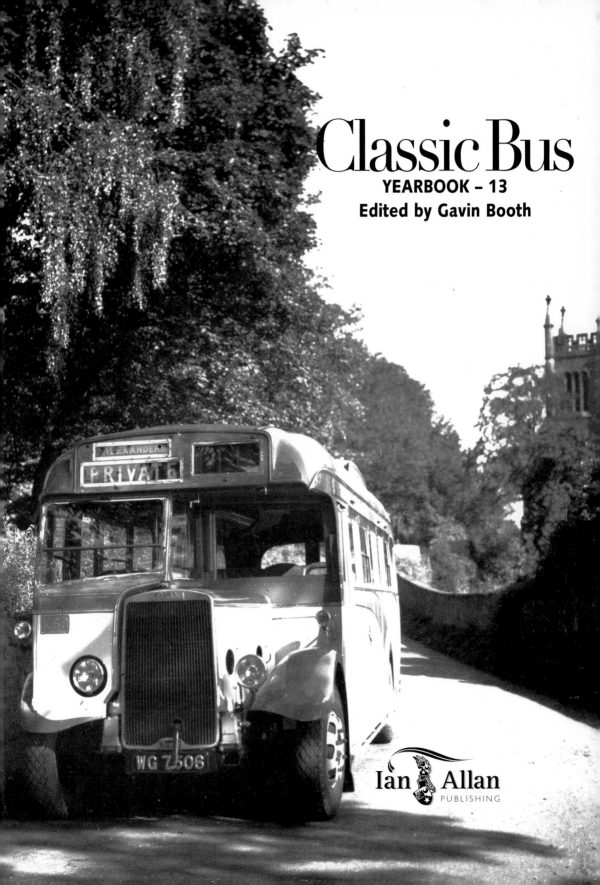

Classic Bus

YEARBOOK – 13

Edited by Gavin Booth

Ian Allan
PUBLISHING

Contents

First published 2007

ISBN (10) 0 7110 3212 2
ISBN (13) 978 0 7110 3212 5

Design by Hieroglyph

Published by Ian Allan Publishing

An imprint of Ian Allan Publishing Ltd, Riverdene Business Park, Molesey Road,
Hersham, Surrey KT12 4RG

Printed by Ian Allan Printing Ltd, Riverdene Business Park, Molesey Road,
Hersham, Surrey KT12 4RG

Visit the Ian Allan Publishing website at www.ianallanpublishing.co.uk

Code: 0703/B1

Introduction

READERS OF THE BI-MONTHLY MAGAZINE *Classic Bus*, have, we know, a wide range of interests, and in this 13th yearbook we offer a suitably varied selection of articles and photo-features contributed by names that will be well-known to all enthusiasts.

Alan Townsin, for instance, the doyen of bus writing, looks back at the 1930s, that decade when the motorbus really came of age and at some of the things that influenced manufacturers and operators.

Geoff Burrows writes on destination displays, from the sublime to the frankly ridiculous. David Wayman covers the Oldham Corporation bus fleet from the end of World War 2 through to the undertaking's disappearance into Selnec PTE, and it is interesting to follow the vehicle-buying policies of a medium-sized municipality.

Michael Dryhurst recalls how many trolleybuses found homes with second owners, usually – but not always – when fleets were abandoning trolleybus operation. David Thrower takes a detailed look at two sometimes-overlooked London single-deck bus types that provided an essential bridge between the surviving prewar types and the first of the new standard RF class – the T and TD types.

Robert E. Jowitt contributes what may be a first in the history of yearbooks like this – a two-part article that starts on these pages and continues later in the year when 'Buses Yearbook 2008' is published.

There is a series of articles on milestones in double-deck design, and there are photo-features on London sightseeing buses, the year 1982, bus rallies over the years, and there are Box Brownie photos from the editor's teenage years, over 40 years ago.

And of course Roger Davies gets the last word – on registration marks, trim, moustaches – and more.

If you enjoy this yearbook, look for the bi-monthly *Classic Bus* magazine; each issue contains some of the best writing and photography around.

Gavin Booth
Edinburgh

Front cover: **Recalling the early days of Selnec PTE, one of the 25 Bristol VRTSL6G with ECW 75-seat bodies ordered by North Western but delivered to Selnec Southern in 1973 and seen at Stockport when new.**
Gavin Booth

Title page: **In his article, Alan Townsin writes about the Leyland Cheetah, the lightweight chassis from the 1930s that was bought by several large fleets, including W. Alexander. This 1938 LZ2A model has Alexander 39-seat bodywork.**

Back cover, upper: **The Bristol/ECW combination was most closely associated with the Tilling Group companies, and passing through Wroxham in 1966 is a 1962 Eastern Counties FS5G 60-seater.**
Back cover, lower: **The PTEs often dual-sourced their vehicle deliveries in the 1970s, and in addition to a substantial fleet of Leyland Atlanteans for Liverpool, Merseyside PTE bought 50 Daimler Fleetline CRG6LXB in 1973, fitted with 75-seat Metro-Cammell bodies for its Wirral Division. No.3044 is outside the former Birkenhead Corporation garage in 1982.**
Both: Gavin Booth

TRIUMPHS AND TROUBLES OF THE 1930s

ALAN TOWNSIN investigates how a complex swirl of influences affected bus design in a difficult economic period, with examples relating to Leyland, Alexander and London Transport

FOR MANY YEARS I'VE FELT THAT BRITAIN was fortunate to have built up a fleet of buses at the outbreak of war in 1939 which mostly gave reliable service until peace returned in 1945 and often ran far beyond the lifespans anticipated when they were built. The typical bus of the early 1920s was barely more advanced in technology than those being built just before the 1914-18 war, but within a few years the leading makers and operators had arrived at models setting the pattern for a further quarter century or more.

It all seemed a fairly orderly progression but in more recent years, hitherto hidden records show that there were many doubts and hesitations even though the few real failures were not built in large numbers. They reveal some surprising cross-currents of influence between seemingly unrelated sources. It is all too easy to fall into the trap of making unfair judgements with the historians' benefit of hindsight. The failures and faltering progress reflected courage in applying new ideas and the willingness to persevere in getting them to work.

Diesel dramas

Diesel-engined buses were first offered for sale in Britain in 1930. In the autumn of 1931 AEC, Gardner and Leyland all announced oil engines in the forms to be built in quantity over the next few years. AEC, after initial troubles, had adopted a new form of indirect injection devised by Ricardo and called the Comet system, accepting rather reluctantly that governing was needed but continuing to aim at quite a free-running engine governed at 2,000rpm or more and giving 130bhp from 8.8 litres, more than any of its contemporaries – and indeed more than most bus operators needed – but it was less economical than direct injection designs. It also required electrical heater plugs for starting from cold, not always easy in severe conditions.

Gardner approached the subject from an opposite viewpoint, only raising the governed speed quite modestly from the 1,300rpm of its 1929 design (originally intended mainly for marine use) to 1,700rpm in its new LW series, allowing 102bhp from the 8.4-litre six-cylinder 6LW. It was now lighter and a

The 'vee-front' style of Leyland double-deck body did not live up to its quite rugged-looking appearance, most requiring extensive rebuilding quite early in life. This example was one of four on Titan TD4c chassis with oil engines and 'Gearless' torque converter transmission supplied to Stockport Corporation in August 1935 and seen in Piccadilly, Manchester a year later. The slim corner pillar at the lower-deck front bulkhead suggests that it had yet to receive attention in this area. However, once properly dealt with, such buses sometimes had long lives – this one remained in service with Stockport until 1959 although, as often the case, a conventional gearbox was fitted just after the war.
G H F Atkins

little less bulky but the version that fitted more readily into a typical bus bonnet was the 5LW, with five cylinders (for many years the only such road-vehicle engine widely available in Britain), 7 litres and giving only 85bhp. The sound of this latter engine in particular, with the firing of individual cylinders easily detectable, was anything but smooth yet fuel economy and reliability were excellent.

Leyland's design was something of a compromise, the original 8-litre version giving barely more power than the 5LW (though running up to 1,900rpm) and falling short of its fuel economy, though bettering AEC's of the time. However, it had the great virtue of being the oil engine that was perhaps the least obtrusive of its era in terms of noise and vibration among those suitable for use in a double-decker.

In a period when the acceptability of oil engines as replacements for the smooth and quiet six-cylinder bus petrol engines of those days was still in doubt, Leyland played a big part in bridging this gulf. Another important related virtue was that the external size was the same as that of the firm's standard petrol engine, so trial installations were readily made by substitution, especially valuable in the depressed economic climate of the time.

Leyland's management seems to have been rather self-conscious about the relatively low output in relation to its capacity of its oil engine. At one stage, serious thought was being given to Leyland following AEC, Crossley and others in adopting the Ricardo Comet form of indirect-injection and indeed a not dissimilar system was adopted for a smaller engine mentioned later.

The London General Omnibus Co Ltd, using AECs, and Manchester Corporation, mainly with Crossleys, were the first major operators to put some numbers of oil-engined buses into daily service from 1931. However, it was the Scottish Motor Traction companies, and in particular W Alexander & Sons Ltd, that were the first of the major British operating concerns covering large areas of the country to adopt diesel buses on a big scale, ordering nearly 300 Leyland engines for conversions in 1933. This was itself not without trouble and even Leyland's 'soft' engine went through a spell of bearing failures – Leyland used a system of sending a service engineer to any garages when oil-engined buses were to be introduced to act as instructors in maintenance methods. Scrupulous cleanliness in regard to fuel injection equipment was just one aspect of an intensive learning process which was needed over the whole industry.

Gardner's progress among bus makers and operators was at first very slow, its name initially almost unknown in this field, quite apart from the uncompromising

A London trolleybus order was both a crisis point and a means of salvation for Leyland's bodybuilding department. Colin Bailey was recruited to produce a much sturdier structure than the 'vee-front' style and the prototype body was delivered on a six-wheel Leyland LPTB70 chassis in April 1936, followed by 100 production examples beginning in Autumn 1937, including no.665, seen here at Uxbridge at the 607 route terminus in postwar days. These vehicles carried their years well, mostly remaining in service until 1960. With a further 325 similar bodies built up to 1940, the LPTB trolleybus department was by far the biggest customer for Leyland bodies during that period.

F G Reynolds

nature of its engine design policy. In 1933 it was chosen for the first bus chassis with oil engine as standard, the Guy Arab, but that model's sales were quite sluggish at that stage, almost ceasing in 1936. The choice of Gardner by Daimler, with the emphasis on municipal fleets, and Bristol, mostly supplying companies associated with the Tilling operating group to which it belonged, were to prove more fruitful but it was not until 1934/35 that demand began to take off. In the case of the Daimler, the fluid flywheel and preselective gearbox helped to 'tame' the Gardner a little. Bristol used a five-speed overdrive gearbox on most of its Gardner-engined single-deckers and this overcame some of the problems of speed limitation as well as improving the fuel economy even further.

It has to be said that the major operating company groups in England and Wales initially had taken a much more cautious line than applied in Scotland. With hindsight, they may have been proved right in cost terms, for much of the money saved by the fuel economy of early diesel buses was at first apt be offset by breakdowns and a need for more engine repairs. It was not until 1935 that the Tilling and British Electric Traction groups began adopting oil engines on a regular basis but it was the pioneer work done by others that had laid the foundations. By July 1935 the SMT group had received some 602 Leyland oil engines for conversions alone.

Bodywork crisis-point

Another aspect of bus design in an unsettled state in the early 1930s was body construction. Metal framing in place of a traditional timber-framed structure offered potential manufacturing cost savings, not least because woodworking craftsmen could be replaced by less expensive use of pressed metal techniques, or so it

doubtless seemed to Leyland and others. That firm's existing body shop was simply allowed to run down, seemingly by quoting fairly high prices, during the earlier part of 1933. No plan for retaining the custom of the many operators who hitherto bought complete Leyland vehicles seems to have been made, which appears surprising as competitors had greatly envied the advantage this offered.

Even a temporary break in supply had obvious dangers when other bodybuilding concerns were hungry for work. Not least was the new Metropolitan-Cammell Weymann set-up created only a few months earlier, providing joint sales and sharing of technology between Metropolitan-Cammell and Weymann, which remained separate firms but jointly grew to become the largest bus bodybuilding organisation in the country.

In the event, it was not until spring 1934 that Leyland began production of its new types of metal-framed bodies, the double-deckers having a distinctive vee-fronted appearance. They were based on standardised frame material supplied by Metal Sections Ltd of Birmingham. Some instances of failures began almost immediately, though at first seemingly overcome without undue trouble. Then, dramatically, in mid-1935 it was reported that there had been 'wholesale breaking-up of all-metal double-deck buses delivered since the beginning of the year' to quote a Leyland management report. It seems ironic that whatever attempts at stress calculations had been made were less effective than the previous methods, based on long experience of timber framing. Earlier timber-framed Leyland bodies remained a familiar sight into the post-1945 period, some surviving for 20 years or more, albeit with some structural renewals at overhaul.

The later prewar style of Leyland metal-framed body proved to be durable, and this lowbridge TD7 supplied to W Alexander in 1941 survived the 1961 split-up of the Alexander company and was finally withdrawn by Alexander (Midland) in 1963.
Gavin Booth

Not long after its formation in 1933 to take over most passenger transport in its area, the London Passenger Transport Board decided to replace its trams with a greatly enlarged trolleybus system. Leyland secured roughly half the orders for chassis. The first batches were being bodied elsewhere but, at the time of its bus body failures, Leyland was committed to supplying a further 100 trolleybuses which were to be complete with Leyland bodies. These were to be to London Transport specification which included a requirement for metal framing and this gave an opportunity for Leyland management to study some being built by Metro-Cammell and to meet Colin Bailey, then in charge of bus body construction with that firm as well as having been a leading light in the development of its very successful metal-framed bus body structure.

Drastic problems needed decisive action; Bailey was persuaded to join Leyland, producing a fresh pillar section avoiding MCW's patent. Far better Leyland body designs, the double-deck motorbus body readily identified by a new curved profile, were put into production in 1936. A major rebuilding programme for the defective bodies was also put in hand at Leyland's expense, the buses being returned to the company's premises at Leyland, Chorley or Kingston.

Barely had it been reported within Leyland in September 1936 that the rebuilding programme was almost complete before fresh reports of trouble with the double-deckers came in. Apparently the front bulkheads had seemed sound at the first overhaul and not then dismantled but quite a number had subsequently failed and, if not caught in time, breakages of pillars spread back along the sides. So a further rebuild was needed, involving visibly thicker lower-deck front bulkhead pillars. In some cases complete new bodies to the curved-front design were supplied.

Customers' confidence was badly damaged by this sequence of events and many major and satisfied users of Leyland chassis, notably big operating companies controlled by BET such as Ribble and Southdown, continued to stay clear of Leyland bodies for the rest of the 1930s, even though the new designs were actually among the most durable then available.

Leyland's body output was thus sometimes below

Top: The Dennis Lancet was a simple model with four-cylinder side-valve petrol engine but perhaps its strongest appeal at a time of recession was its low price, causing some alarm to the management of competitors by attracting orders from major operators such as Eastern National, to whom this example was one of 30 supplied in 1933, this one remaining in service until 1950. The 36-seat body was by Eastern Counties, whose bodybuilding department became a separate business under the name of Eastern Coach Works in 1936.
Eastern Counties

Above: An early attempt to regain the lower-priced end of the single-deck market was to use a version of the lightweight six-cylinder Leyland Cub model with long wheelbase and forward-control layout. Alexander's S14 (WG 1618) was one of a pair with Alexander 32-seat bodywork dating from June 1933. The other similar bus, S13, was chosen to receive one of the first of a new type of 4.7-litre oil engine in August 1935. It was reported to Leyland as giving a good performance, perhaps benefiting from being a hand-built prototype and the vehicle doubtless quite light, thus encouraging the placing of large orders for the new Cheetah model introduced a few months later.
Leyland

AEC's venture into a lighter class of model was the Regal Mark II (type 0862), although it was only marginally lighter than the standard Regal of the day the main difference being the new '6.6-litre' engine. This was the first one, chassis number 0862001. Externally the main recognition feature was the smaller radiator with chromium-plated shell and vertical slats, these latter features not then found on other AEC models. Weymann built the 32-seat body and it was supplied to the Rhondda Transport Co Ltd after display at the 1935 Show. The A 172 engine, with true volume of 6.75 litres, was disastrously troublesome in its original form. AEC

capacity during this period, often being dominated by trolleybuses for London. The second most regular users were the companies in the SMT group, even though they too had received defective bodies in 1934/35. For a time municipal orders were on a small scale, largely from modest-sized undertakings in Lancashire. Ironically, even Alexander cancelled an order which was to include the first of the new-style double-deck bus bodies in the spring of 1936 (this going to the Swan fleet in Swansea) but they and the various SMT companies again became regular users from soon afterwards, many of the bodies then supplied surviving into the 1960s. Increasingly Alexander was drawn into closer cooperation with Leyland in relation to bodywork matters. When Leyland was unable to build bus bodies in wartime and in the immediate aftermath, Alexander's body department built what amounted to Leyland bodies.

Lightweight nightmares

The depression years had increased pressure for new lighter and cheaper bus models. It seems that Leyland was quite taken aback by the success of the Dennis Lancet, introduced as an inexpensive single-decker at the 1931 Show at a startling introductory chassis price of £595. Its design was a modest revamp of the Dennis E of the late 1920s but it was given a bold and distinctive appearance, collecting orders from several of the larger company fleets as well as independents and taking business from the Leyland Lion model of the day, the LT5. Leyland took a little too long to decide on its answer, in the form of the LT5A with its modernised appearance, and some

more business was lost because lack of parts caused delays in delivery in early 1934.

As it turned out, both AEC and Leyland went through new waves of trouble concerning lighter diesel-engined single-deckers announced at the Commercial Vehicle Show of November 1935. AEC had already made one step in that direction, introducing a more compact replacement for the 8.8-litre oil engine. This was the unit always known as the '7.7-litre' although most examples were really of 7.58 litres, going into general production from the latter part of 1934. It was adopted for the standard London double-decker of the mid-1930s, the STL type, and was to go through its own troubles but ultimately was to be built in vast numbers until the mid-1950s.

However, for the new lighter AEC Regal Mark II single-decker (model 0862), a further new six-cylinder engine, planned to be cheaper to make and called the 6.6-litre, though again actually of a slightly different true volume of 6.75 litres, was introduced. The cylinder block and crankcase were combined into one casting, with what were called 'wet' liners for each cylinder, in direct contact with the cooling water and sealed by rubber rings. However, there was soon a disastrous amount of trouble, including seizures and destructive bearing failures.

After about 60 production chassis were built in 1936, mainly for BET companies, Regal II output seems suddenly to have stopped. A petrol-engined version of the model was introduced and 34 of these were built up to 1939. A few more oil-engined Regal II were built in 1938/39, and there was a military version of the engine used in pairs in tanks, evidently with the main problems overcome. The concept was not pursued further at that stage although its main features were revived in the 1950s for the AH410 and 470 engines used in early examples of the underfloor-engined Reliance model.

Leyland's lightweight single-decker also introduced at the 1935 Show went much further in trimming vehicle weight, its design roots taken from the smaller Cub range of models in the 20-24-seat class and built at the firm's Kingston-on-Thames works. An initial longer forward-control version was sometimes called the Lion Cub but this proved underpowered as a 32-seater with the early Cub 4.4-litre side-valve petrol engine. Redesign of that engine to 4.7-litre size with overhead valves and of the chassis, giving appearance much like the contemporary Lion LT7 (similar to the LT5A) though with Cub-family axles, produced a new model called the Cheetah.

It was reported at the end of 1935 that SMT had ordered 300 Cheetah oil-engined buses. Alexander produced a new full-fronted metal-framed bus body

for them, with grille concealing the radiator. Structurally, the 4.7-litre diesel engine was effectively to the same basic design as the new petrol unit, a bit on the light side because of its history, but using an indirect-injection system intended as Leyland's answer to the Ricardo Comet, and tending to run a bit hotter than direct-injection engines.

Production manufacture of Cheetah chassis started in December 1935, the plan being that eight oil engines per week were to be supplied by Kingston to the main works at Leyland, where the Cheetah chassis were being assembled. However, ominous reports of weak engine castings and big-end failures of 4.7-litre oil engines on test began that same month. Prudently as it turned out, the SMT group order was reduced to 100 by February 1936 though it seems that at least part of the remainder were deferred rather than cancelled.

In April, engine failures were being reported very soon after the first buses were delivered. The original plan was for Alexander to receive the first 20 of the group's Cheetah buses, at least one getting as far as being painted accordingly. In the event they were transferred to Western SMT, who also took 20 more,

Both Leyland and the SMT group had high hopes for the Leyland Cheetah and its 4.7-litre oil engine, derived along with many of its chassis features from components designed for the Cub range. This picture shows what was to have been the first of 20 supplied to Alexander, the fleet and registration numbers being reserved as K1-20 (WG 3492-3511). In the event, these vehicles, of type LZ2, were transferred to Western SMT before registration, being recorded as delivered in April-May 1936 and registered in the CS series; the above WG registration numbers were used for new Leyland Tigers later in 1936. The Alexander bodywork seated 37.

while 60 went to the parent Scottish Motor Traction Co Ltd, all delivered by August 1936.

Complete replacement engines to replace broken-down units were needed quite frequently to keep these buses in service and by May two or three engines per week were being supplied directly to Scotland – in the rebuilding process the engine casings were being replaced by a sturdier design. The Kingston works was struggling to keep up with the rebuilding of the returned engines and the supply of oil engines for new Cheetah chassis assembly at Leyland almost ceased.

By August, a minimum of four oil engines per week were being sent to Scotland. Gradually the troubles were overcome but a good deal of damage to the firm's reputation had been done as well as a substantial drain on its resources. Lessons were learnt and a more cautious approach to testing of new engine designs became evident thereafter. In a remarkably close parallel to the situation with the AEC Regal Mark II, only a few oil-engined Cheetah models were built after 1936 although the petrol version was far more successful, becoming Ribble's standard choice of bus for use in the more rural parts of its territory, for instance. Alexander did eventually take 90 Cheetahs with halfcab bodies in 1938 but they were petrol-engined as built, though with one final and significant exception. The last of the batch received a prototype of a new 6.2-litre oil engine which was designed in part to benefit from the hard lessons taught by the 4.7-litre episode, as well as being meant to some degree as

Alexander and the closely-associated David Lawson fleet did receive some Cheetah models in 1938 but these were petrol-engined LZ2A models as built and received more conventional halfcab bodies. Seen here is K48 (WG 7486) with Alexander 39-seat body in 'Bluebird' livery. In later years, many of these vehicles received 7.4-litre oil engines, this one in 1947.

Leyland's answer to the 5LW. It was known as the L-type, intended for a new range of models, including a new Lion Six single-decker, type LSI, which the war prevented from going into production. However, the design was adapted for military uses and eventually developed into the 7.4-litre engine standard in the post-war Titan PD1 and Tiger PS1 standard models.

Unintended consequences

Another result of a study of those days is the realisation that unlikely-seeming influences could help to steer later policy. As indicated above, Leyland's management was uneasy about the modest output of its standard pot-cavity oil engine, initially of 8-litre and, from 1934, 8.6-litre capacity.

However, contact with London Transport led to the discovery that A A M Durrant, Chief Engineer (Buses and Coaches) of that organisation, was greatly impressed with the 'pot' engine, a few of which were being run in ex-independent Leyland Titans. Hitherto, direct-injection engines had been ruled out for use on buses in central London because of their noise level

Previous page: **Leyland liked to have something new and controversial on display at the Commercial Vehicle Show to attract trade visitors. For the 1937 event, it was the first example of the Gnu TEP1 single-decker, built for and bodied by Alexander to a suitably eye-catching style. The frontal appearance owed much to that of a new Greyhound coach introduced the previous year in the United States and reputedly designed in the large and then quite new General Motors styling department.**

Above: **The entrance of the Alexander-bodied Gnu reveals a wide driver's cab area and a single seat on the nearside.**

and harshness (a view no doubt formed on the basis of small-scale running of Gardner 6LW engines in a few early AEC Renown six-wheelers), but the Leyland engine had changed his view. London experience also favoured deliberately 'derating' engines – in other words, setting them to give a slightly lower than maximum output, so as to improve reliability.
No doubt learning of such views helped Leyland to become more self-confident in the mid-1930s, as did very healthy sales figures for 8.6-litre engined buses.

Operating experience of the 100 Titan TD4 buses placed in service by London Transport as its STD class in 1937 led Durrant to the view that the 8.6-litre engine with which they were fitted was an improvement over the standard AEC product of the time, the 7.7-litre AEC, then still in its indirect-injection form. When AEC had been separated off and made an independent concern in 1933 as part of the setting-up process for the newly formed London Transport, it was agreed that LT would be required to obtain most of its buses from AEC for ten years. From 1938 a special version of the AEC 8.8-litre engine was built using the Leyland pot cavity system, built under licence. This was used on the 266 Green Line coaches built in 1938, best-known as the 10T10 type, and for large-scale conversions of the LT-class of AEC Renown six-wheel double-deckers of 1931/32 which continued into wartime.

Meanwhile there was close co-operation between Leyland and London Transport in the design of a new type of coach, also to be used mainly for Green Line duty, beginning with a meeting held at Chiswick in January 1936. Eric Ottaway, who was Durrant's right-hand man in terms of vehicle design, became a regular visitor to Leyland and it is clear that what became best known by its London Transport designation, the TF type (although Leyland designated it FEC, signifying 'Flat Engine Coach'), was very much a joint effort. This was the first British bus or coach design having a horizontal underfloor engine, a suitably modified

Going through Leyland's design department at the same time as the Gnu was the prototype of a coach built for London Transport and best-known by the latter's designation TF; it was the first British bus or coach to go into production with an underfloor engine. There was some mutual influence in the chassis design of the two designs but the LPTB adopted the unusual concept of using what almost amounted to a halfcab front-end to improve the driver's vision to the left, as shown in this view of TF16 from the production batch of Green Line coaches of 1939, seen in 1952 when demoted to a local country area service from St Albans. E J Smith

version of the 8.6-litre unit. This in turn required a fairly high frame level and, unusually at the time, straight side-members were adopted instead of dipping between the axles as was then usual. Construction of the prototype began later that year.

Independently, Leyland was investigating a series of ideas on vehicles of unorthodox layout and indeed Eric Ottaway was shown a rear-engined prototype that had been built when he visited Leyland in February 1936.

By September that year, it had been decided to build what was at first called the 'Dual Six Tiger' which had two steering axles (each of these basically as used on the Cheetah, incidentally). Although having what was then a conventional upright 8.6-litre engine, the radiator and fan were to be offset to one side to allow the engine to be mounted well forward, thereby accommodating a body which could seat up to 43 passengers within the 30ft length which was permissible for it at that date as a three-axle vehicle – two-axle single-deckers operating in Britain were limited to 27ft 6in until 1950. Here again the frame was straight, with a floor height of 3ft – the wording of the original description makes it clear that this aspect of the twin-steering model followed the London Transport flat-engined model then in hand. By the end of 1936, it had been agreed that this vehicle, later christened the Gnu, would be supplied to and bodied by Alexander and indeed two such buses were completed in 1937.

Later, the twin-steer chassis was itself developed with underfloor engine position. It had been intended to show the resulting Panda model at the 1939 Show that was cancelled although it was subsequently bodied by Alexander and delivered to the operating department of that concern in September 1941.

A further intriguing project that was discussed was the possibility that London Transport might take some twin-steer versions of the TF coach for use on routes where greater seating capacity was needed, but again the war intervened and the idea was never pursued. However, there was another instance of common ground between Leyland, Alexander and London Transport in the use of the twin-steering layout for a prototype trolleybus supplied to LPTB in 1939 but the war killed any further progress on this, too. **CB**

MILESTONES IN DOUBLE-DECK BUS DESIGN

GAVIN BOOTH looks at significant types

The Leyland Titan TD1

Was there life before the TD1?

Yes indeed. From Day One the motorbus was seen as a largely urban animal and even then London made the running for the rest of the country. The city's spectacular growth in the second half of the 19th century meant that London entered the 20th century with a huge fleet of double-deck horsebuses. London's first proper motorbuses were clearly descended from the horsebuses, their bodies mounted high above the ground with an open staircase at the back and an open top deck. The big difference, of course, was that the driver no longer controlled horses but an engine mounted in front of him that produced horse power in a very different way.

Then, as now, London was by far the biggest single market for motorbuses, so developments were usually driven by London operators. If the London General B type represented the first motorbus regarded as totally reliable and suitable for London conditions, the 1919 K type was an important stage in the evolutionary process by moving the driver alongside the engine, releasing more space for seated passengers – 46 of them rather than 34. Then the 1923 NS type took things a stage further with its lower-built chassis, making buses more passenger-friendly. But the progress of London's buses was rather stymied by the Metropolitan Police, who wouldn't allow pneumatic tyres on the NS until 1928, covered tops until after 1925, and windscreens for drivers until 1931. The first bus that successfully pulled together the various strands of double-deck development, then, was Leyland's 1927 Titan TD1.

So, what was different about the TD1?

While the London General NS improved by evolution, the TD1 represented a revolution. Leyland's previous

The Titan's predecessors were buses like the 1922 Short-bodied G7 on the right, although the 1929 Titan TD1 on the left is hardly typical with its open-top Brush body. Both were Southdown buses, now in Stagecoach's heritage fleet.
Gavin Booth

attempts at double-deckers had often been ungainly and – in contrast to the TD1 – fairly primitive. The TD1 was designed from the ground up as an all-new bus with a low-slung chassis, a lightweight low-height (13ft, 3.96m) 48-seat top-covered body, pneumatic tyres and a six-cylinder petrol engine.

The result was a bus that in general outline was to set the pattern for the next 30 years. Outside London it succeeded in convincing many operators and passengers that double-deck buses could be safely operated as the answer to fast-growing bus services. And not just in towns and cities but on interurban duties.

One slightly anachronistic feature of the TD1 was the open staircase at the rear, but fully-enclosed versions followed from 1929.

The TD1 achieved its low height with its offside side gangway and four-across seating arrangement on the upper deck, a layout that would soon become widely described as lowbridge. From 1929 a 14ft (4.26m) Hybridge version was also offered.

The TD1 was followed in fairly quick succession by the TD2, TD3, TD4, TD5 and TD7, each new designation representing an improvement on its predecessors in an era when technical advances came thick and fast. The most significant development was the diesel engine, offered from 1932 but becoming all but standard from 1935. Leyland also experimented with a semi-automatic 'Gearless' torque converter transmission from 1933. The 'missing' TD6 Titan was actually the TD6c, a special version with torque converter built for Birmingham City Transport.

Leyland's body style changed too, from the distinctive 'piano-front' body on the TD1 and TD2 to a less than successful vee-fronted metal-framed body on the TD3 from 1934, to the classic style worn by models from the 1936 TD4 onwards.

The last front-engined Leyland Titans, PD3/14 models delivered in 1969, were very different buses to the TD1, and yet it is easy to trace their ancestry over the Titan's 42-year life.

Where Leyland went, did others follow?

Of course, and Leyland's biggest rival, AEC, managed to poach the TD1's legendary designer, G. J. Rackham, to help it develop big six-cylinder engines, and the Regent/Regal family that would rival Leyland's Titan and single-deck Tiger for 40 years. Other manufacturers were slower to follow Leyland's lead, but Bristol and Daimler, plus a raft of smaller manufacturers, had viable competing models by the mid-1930s, though AEC and Leyland dominated the market. With its interest in

Top: **Titan TD1s often enjoyed long lives. This 1931 Crosville example was still in the fleet in 1954, when the North Western & Yorkshire Branch of The Omnibus Society hired it for a study tour.**

Above: **The Titan quickly developed in the 1930s, and this 1934 TD3 for Samuel Ledgard carries the early metal-framed Leyland body style that caused many problems, as recounted in Alan Townsin's article in this book.**

AEC, London Transport went for the Regent as its standard double-deck model in the 1930s, while Leyland picked up much municipal and company business. Daimler, offering a preselective gearbox as standard, won substantial orders from Birmingham City Transport and became a municipal favourite. **CB**

GOING MY WAY?

GEOFF BURROWS considers the many ways that bus operators have provided destination information, and with varying degrees of success and legibility

'YOU GET WHAT IT SAYS ON THE TIN', THE TV commercial says. Apply it to today's buses, and you don't get much, certainly when it comes to destination information.

In the early days of bus operation, the names of the places served were carefully painted on to the buses, but as soon as the operators grew in size and began to work more routes, this simple method could not be used. The next step was the use of removable destination boards, until technological improvement in the form of roller blinds took over. This phase came about during the 1920s, and the displays then became very simple, with the destination shown alone on a single line, sometimes with a route number alongside.

This was never the case in London, where a feature of the capital's buses was the large amount of information shown about the routes served – though as

The narrow single-line destination box was a feature of the Sunderland District buses until 1950, illustrated here by no.174, a Roe-bodied Leyland TD7.
Geoff Burrows

this aspect of London's buses has been written about many times elsewhere, we can move on. This did not go unnoticed in the rest of the country and gradually other operators began to realise the importance of advertising what they had for sale. In other words, show the public not only where their buses were going, but also by what route. And so it seems that the word 'via' came into use in the bus world.

One of the first operators to use separate destination and 'via' blinds was Wallasey Corporation, where two equally-sized indicators were placed one

Birmingham Corporation blended a single destination display into its unique body design. No.2319 was one of the first Crossleys for the fleet, new in 1949 with Crossley body.
Geoff Burrows

above the other on its six Karrier DD6 double-deckers of 1928. The following year saw the delivery of a batch of similarly equipped Leyland-bodied TD1s, and in 1930 three Daimler CF6s and three Leylands with Eastwood & Kenning were the first in the fleet to receive the addition of route number blinds. The boxes for these were neatly placed to the right of the destination and route boxes, on both the front and rear of the buses. This arrangement set the pattern in Wallasey until the end of corporation ownership, though the sizes changed over the years.

Neighbouring Birkenhead operated several joint services with Wallasey, and halfway through a delivery of Leyland Titans in 1928 changed from the single–line destination indicator fitted as standard to Leyland bodies to the same 'twin-box' arrangement that Wallasey had adopted. More similar buses followed until 1931, when a route-numbering scheme came into operation jointly with Wallasey. To accommodate the route numbers, twin number boxes were fitted inside the front upper deck windows. It was not until 1934 that Birkenhead received any buses with the route number boxes 'built-in'. They were placed centrally, above the twin destination and route

number boxes. This layout was retained until 1938, when for all subsequent deliveries of new buses the route numbers were moved to the side, making the layout the same as Wallasey.

Imitation of this layout meant that eventually it was to become one of the most common forms to be found among the municipal operators. The size and shape varied, of course, though there were examples of identical displays, for instance Newcastle and Huddersfield, where the manager had moved from one to the other during the furtherance of his career. Stalybridge, Hyde, Mossley & Dukinfield Joint Board used a very small version, and the route numbers were barely large enough to read.

Very few company operators adopted this layout, and in most cases only for a few years of use. Tilling companies Eastern National, Hants & Dorset and Southern Vectis are examples of these, where quite

neat versions were fitted to both single- and double-deckers. The Northern Ireland Road Transport Board had this layout, giving a commonality with Belfast Corporation. In England, the largest of the BET companies, Midland Red, adopted this system universally from 1945.

Variation

A variation of the three-box system placed the number blind in the centre directly over the other two as in the original Birkenhead arrangement. This was used for a time at Dundee, Glasgow and Sheffield, but found little favour elsewhere. It was difficult for coachbuilders to fit it in without compromising the body structure, and the arrangements to bring the winding handles to a convenient position were mechanically quite complicated. Many operators preferred to incorporate the destination and 'via' points in one rectangular box underneath the route number.

The three-box system came near to perfection in Manchester in 1936. Designed for use in the new 'Streamliner' bodies, the ultimate single line destination was placed centrally at the top. Below on the left was a large rectangular two-track number box, and to the right of this a 'via' box of the same shape and size with three highly legible lines of names. Apart from Rochdale and latterly Lancashire United this symmetrical, well-proportioned layout had few other imitators.

Blackpool used two equal-sized deep rectangular

Above: **Edinburgh Corporation used the full 'double-deck' indicators to good effect on Leyland-bodied Royal Tiger no.813. Edinburgh's present-day successor, Lothian Buses, still specifies a comprehensive blind display on its fleet.**
Geoff Burrows

Opposite above: **Hastings no.10, a Weymann-bodied Sunbeam with single aperture box shows the destination, the 'via' points and a circle surrounding the route number.**
Geoff Burrows

Left: **The classic 'three-box' indicator is displayed by Birkenhead Leyland PD2/East Lancs no.386.**
Geoff Burrows

boxes placed side by side, the offside one showed the destination and an intermediate point, the nearside displayed a large route number. The slightly vee-front flat panels of the unique Blackpool-designed bodies allowed this arrangement, which occupied the full width of the bus.

In Liverpool, where a new fleet of AEC buses had begun to enter service in 1935, what could be termed a 'traditional' layout, with the destination and 'via' point on the left and a square route number on the right. The new Liverpool streamlined 'Green Goddess' trams, though, had an entirely different arrangement. First seen in 1936, they had two large rectangular

This Weymann-bodied Daimler COG5, Dundee no.106, is fitted with that municipality's version of the 'three box' indicator.
Geoff Burrows collection

The short Sunbeam MF2B chassis, front entrance/centre exit Roe body, trolley retrievers, streamlined livery and service number with route box but without final destination indicators were all unique features at Kingston upon Hull, shown here on 'Coronation' trolleybus no.103.
Geoff Burrows

displays, with the destination on the left and the intermediate places on the right. The design was completed with a huge route number box mounted centrally above these.

In the early postwar days Liverpool wanted to show the same display on the buses that were bought to replace the trams. There was insufficient space for this on the 7ft 6in-wide buses of that era, and a compromise solution saw a single destination/route box in the centre, surmounted by a route number box. When 8ft-wide buses became available, it became possible to achieve the 'tram' layout, but only by introducing a slightly flattened front panel and reducing the radius of the corners.

Traditional

Meanwhile, most operators adopted either the 'traditional' layout, or used a large rectangular box, to show the route number, destination and passing points all on one comprehensive display. Some were arranged to show one destination at the top of the display; by winding the blind up a few turns this was hidden, and the name at the other end of the route was then exposed at the bottom. These became known as 'lazy blinds'.

The 'tin bible' clipped to the front of the bus was used by several Tilling companies. It comprised a metal plate with the names painted on; a hinge in the middle enabled the plate to be turned over to show the other terminus. Crosville buses used the destination

box to show the company name! A 'Widd' plate, a plastic card held against the front bulkhead glass with a spring holder, was used instead to show the destination. Single line indicators remained in use with a few operators, the largest and best known was Birmingham, where normally only the outer terminus was shown. The 'Clayton' box was used mainly by BET companies; there were spare blinds inside that could be changed when a bus was moved from its home depot to another.

Among the operators that maintained a singular approach to destination displays, two are worth mentioning here. On the Kingston upon Hull trolleybus fleet, a large rectangular number display above a small single line 'via' blind was considered sufficient. Note that I said 'via' blind – the destination was not shown! This arrangement was in use from 1947 until the end of the trolleybus era there. At Ipswich, all the trolleybuses ever owned by the corporation had a display that was almost square, being just a little higher

Above: Ipswich trolleybus no.69 displays 'Station X' on the oddly-proportioned indicator. The side destination box was also unusually positioned on this Massey-bodied Ransomes vehicle.
Geoff Burrows

Below: The first batch of full-fronted centre entrance Leyland/Burlingham double-deckers in the Blackpool fleet included no.141, with the distinctive twin destination/via and route number indicators.
Geoff Burrows

The tram-derived destination equipment layout in Liverpool was well suited to the Leyland Atlantean buses in that city. L677 was bodied by Metro-Cammell.
Geoff Burrows

Resplendent in Hants & Sussex livery, this Bedford OB illustrates a
good example of a comprehensive destination, route and number
blind. This is not the 'lazy' variety!

Geoff Burrows

than wide. And it wasn't very wide, just large enough to show a single digit number, and the destination in small letters.

Rather than try to describe all the variations that have been used, this is simply a brief outline of some of the most significant developments. It has been written in the hope that the reader will take another look at the many different examples seen in photographs, and see what a wide variation there was. Neither is it an attempt to go into the many different displays used on the sides and backs of buses. It would need another article to do these justice, and yet another for single-deckers and coaches.

There remains one relevant design to be discussed, used by the largest number of buses both single and double deck, outside the capital. The Tilling Group introduced a standard layout in 1945, and most readers will be familiar with the wide box showing the destination over an equally wide box showing the route and number. At first identical displays were used over the entrance and at the rear, but these were soon abandoned and removed or painted over. Then the route number was given a separate box and the 'via' box reduced in width to accommodate this. Even this arrangement was gradually given up, due to a combination of economy drives and the reluctance of crews to use them correctly.

This was the beginning of the end of comprehensive destination displays, that eventually led to today's simple destination and number side by side, which is where we came in! **CB**

NEW BRIGHTON
VIA SEABANK ROAD

FHF 451

Where it all started? The layout used by Wallasey is shown on preserved no.1, one of the very first Leyland Atlanteans to be built.
Geoff Burrows

Above: The Scottish Bus Group devised its own variation of the route number over destination box, though it owed much to an earlier Ribble layout. This ECW-bodied Leyland Fleetline in the Midland Scottish fleet waits to turn left in Perth.
Geoff Burrows

Below: One of the many versions of the simplified postwar Tilling destination screens was the 'T' layout. Wilts & Dorset OHR 919 shows this to good effect.
Geoff Burrows

MILESTONES IN DOUBLE-DECK BUS DESIGN

GAVIN BOOTH considers an all-time classic

The AEC Regent RT

Was there life before the RT?

The RT represented the culmination of London Transport's double-deck development in the 1930s. London General had opted for AEC's Regent as its standard double-decker as far back as 1930, the ST type, with batches of the LT type three-axle AEC Renown thrown in for good measure from 1929 onwards. The ST paved the way for the longer STL in 1932, and following the creation of the new London Passenger Transport Board in 1933, what had become London Transport set about ridding itself of what now seemed outmoded 1920s types and building up a highly-standardised fleet. As it evolved, the STL represented the bridge between the petrol-engined ST and the RT that would succeed it. In its seven-year production span, the STL developed into a diesel-engined bus with a preselective gearbox and the RT took this concept an important step further.

So, what was different about the RT?

Where to start? London Transport and AEC took all the best features of the STL and added a big 9.6-litre engine, air pressure brakes, an air pressure-operated gearbox and a fluid flywheel. At first RT1 was disguised with a 1932 body from a Leyland Titan acquired with the business of an independent operator, but in February 1939 it was launched with a stylish new body design that many might argue has never been bettered.

The low-slung AEC radiator and deep driver's cab windows marked it as clearly different from anything else on the market. There were just four window bays

Photographed in 1950, newly-delivered RT1878 and a new RTL on tram-replacement duties.

Against an unusual backdrop, RT2565 poses at South Queensferry with the Forth Bridge behind, while in Scotland for a transport conference.

between the bulkheads rather than the more popular five (and occasionally six) favoured at the time. Roe had built deep-windowed four-bay bodywork for Leeds City Transport, but it would be in the late 1940s before four-bay bodies would become more common – and some builders stuck with five-bay bodies to the end.

But development of the RT had to be put on hold with the outbreak of war just seven months after RT1 was revealed to the world. Another 150 RTs were built in the early war years, all with bodies built by LPTB at its Chiswick Works, but wartime shortages forced production to stop until hostilities ceased. Plans to order around 500 a year from 1940 onwards were abandoned.

London Transport had been in the forefront of technical development in the late 1930s, leading the way in engine and gearbox technology and experimenting with underfloor-engined and rear-engined single-deckers, but these also took to the streets in 1939 and it would be another 12 years before LT would return to underfloor-engined buses, and another 26 years before it revisited rear-engined types.

When RT production resumed after the war, in 1947, it was a rather different beast, partly as a result of LT's wartime involvement in the production of aircraft at its Chiswick and Aldenham works. Mass-production using jig-built components was seen as the way to ensure that bodies and chassis could be interchanged and that parts could be standardised. The postwar RTs looked broadly similar to their 'prewar' brothers; the most notable difference was the rectangular driver's windscreen. But they differed under the skin. Although RT1 had a metal-framed body, the other 'prewar' buses had composite wood/metal bodies. The postwar bodies would be

virtually all-metal and were mainly built by Park Royal and Weymann, with batches by Craven and Saunders. To speed production while LT replaced time-expired prewar buses and unsuitable wartime ones – and to complete the tram replacement programme – RT-type buses were also built by Leyland (RTL type) with bodies by Park Royal and Weymann, as well as by Metro-Cammell. The Metro-Cammell bodies were not interchangeable with other RT/RTL bodies, unlike the Park Royal and Weymann examples.

The last RTs and RTLs were delivered to LT late in 1954, by which time the combined classes totalled 6,456 vehicles, the largest quantity of near-identical buses delivered to a UK operator. By the time the last RTs and RTLs were entering service, in 1958/59, some older examples of the types were being withdrawn, and indeed the Routemaster, the next generation of London double-decker, was entering squadron service.

The last RTs ran in London service in 1979.

Where AEC went, did others follow?

Up to a point, yes. The idea of using derated bigger capacity engines was widely adopted after World War 2, and preselective gearboxes were often specified. The need for interchangeable bodies was really a London thing, although a few operators bought what were essentially London-style RTs. Others bought RT chassis with other types of body, but many more went for the RT's provincial brother, the Regent III. Something close to the RT body design was produced by Park Royal for other operators, and there was a widespread move to all-metal bodies in the 1950s. And just as the experience with the STL had influenced the RT family, experience with the RT led to the Routemaster in the 1950s and 1960s. **CB**

AN OPEN AND CLOSED CASE

Sightseeing tours of London have been provided by a wide range of buses, both closed-top and open-top. GEOFF RIXON's photographs recall some of these

In the days before London sightseeing tours became really big business, an April 1978 view at the junction of Victoria Street and Buckingham Palace Road, with the unique rear-engined Routemaster, FRM1, and former Bournemouth Daimler Fleetline/Weymann, DMO6, both on Round London Sightseeing Tour duties.

All photos by Geoff Rixon

Above: **The preserved 1925 Dennis 4-ton with 48-seat Dodson body, D142, on tourist duties turning into Regent Street at Oxford Circus in April 1980.**

Below: **Prince Marshall's Obsolete Fleet acquired some ex-Midland Red BMMO D9s, which were hired to London Transport for sightseeing work. This is BM9 rounding Hyde Park Corner in April 1981.**

Above: **The prototype Scania/MCW Metropolitan in Park Lane on sightseeing work for Globus Gateway in June 1981.**

Below: **Open-top London Country Leyland Atlantean/Metro-Cammell, AN110, on RLST duties at Hyde Park Corner in July 1982.**

Above: **Straightforward fare on the RLST in September 1981, Stockwell garage's Leyland Fleetline, DM2646, in Parliament Square.**

Right: **Culture Bus** pioneered the hop-on-hop-off style of sightseeing tour using buses like this former London Transport Daimler Fleetline.

Above: **A bus with rather more character was this 1949 ex-Morecambe & Heysham Corporation AEC Regent III/Park Royal, KTF 591, in use with Ebdon's Tours, Sidcup, in Whitehall in July 1984.**

Below: **Newly-delivered London Transport MCW Metrobus, M1053, on RLST duties leaving Whitehall in August 1984.**

Above: **Fresh from Aldenham Works in May 1986, London Transport former coach Routemaster, RCL2248, turns into the Centre Road at Marble Arch.**

Left: **Another former Routemaster coach, RCL2243, converted to partly open-top layout, sports a McDonalds overall livery, enters the Haymarket from Coventry Street on sightseeing work in June 1993.**

Above: The varied career of rear-engined Routemaster, FRM1, included a spell on sightseeing duties; here it passes Marble Arch in July 1982.

Below: Ten Routemasters were extended for sightseeing work, the ERM class, and ERM281 is working on Arriva's Original Tour at Marble Arch in July 2001. All ten were bought by Lothian Buses for its Mac Tours operation in Edinburgh.

Above: **Big Bus** was using this former Northern General forward entrance Routemaster, which it numbered RMF592. It is at Hyde Park Corner in February 2003.

Right: **An interesting** conversion of a former London Buses Daimler Fleetline, DMS1935, in use on a hop-on-hop-off tour in Whitehall in June 1994. Note the canopy top and the offside door.

MEMORIES OF 1982

GAVIN BOOTH digs out some of the photos he took 25 years ago, in 1982

Above: **Three generations of Newcastle double-decker caught together at the Dunbar Rally in 1982 – from left, a 1962 Leyland Atlantean PDR1/1 with Alexander 78-seat body, a 1980 Atlantean AN68A/2R with Alexander 78-seat body, and a new Scania BR112DH, again with Alexander 78-seat body.**
All photos by Gavin Booth

Left: **The Bus & Coach Council, forerunners of today's Confederation of Passenger Transport, mounted a campaign on the theme 'We'd all miss the bus', and BCC members painted buses in this overall scheme. This is a new West Midlands PTE MCW Metrobus, at Walsall.**

Above: Leyland introduced its new Olympian model in 1980 and by 1982 deliveries were beginning to increase. This is a long-wheelbase Olympian, one of two delivered in 1982 to Warrington Borough Council with 88-seat East Lancs bodywork, seen in August.

Below: Not far away, Merseyside PTE was still buying its trusted Leyland Atlantean AN68D/1R with 76-seat Alexander bodies. This newly-delivered example is on a private hire in Liverpool city centre in August.

Above: **Greater Manchester PTE** was also still buying Atlanteans, AN68D/1R models with Northern Counties 75-seat bodies. Note the different glazing on newly-delivered no.8541 and slightly older no.8289, in Wigan in August.

Left: **Greater Manchester** was also keeping its options open for future double-deck deliveries, and was building up a substantial fleet of MCW Metrobuses, like recently-delivered no.5127 in Piccadilly, Manchester, in June.

Above: National Bus Company fleets were still buying Leyland's trusty Leopard, and this United Counties PSU3G/4R model with ECW B51-style 49-seat body, is seen in April at Victoria Coach Station, London, on National Express duties.

Below: Crosville was also buying Leopards, but this newly-delivered PSU3E/4R, at Chorlton Street, Manchester in August, has a 47-seat Willowbrook body.

Above: New deliveries to Lothian Region Transport in my hometown of Edinburgh were unusually mixed, and included 18 of these unusual Leyland Cub CU435 with Duple Dominant 31-seat bodies in 1981. Normally used on lighter duties, here in October 1982 no.171 looks as if it could be overwhelmed by the Princes Street bus queue when it appears on a 'big bus' route.

Below: More substantial single-deck deliveries for Lothian in 1982 were its first four Leyland Nationals, with two-door 45-seat bodies. One is seen at Craighouse, Edinburgh, in April.

After buying a steady diet of Leyland Atlanteans since 1965, Lothian tried two of the new Olympians in 1982, ONTL11/R examples with Alexander R type bodies. Note the unusual electronic blind display on no.666, at Granton in April.

Above: Unusual deliveries to Scottish Bus Group's Eastern Scottish fleet were five Bedford VAS5 with Reeve Burgess 17-seat bodies, fitted with rear luggage compartments for the Border Courier services in the Scottish Borders. ZC10D is at Galashiels in April.

Below: At the other end of the single-deck scale for Eastern Scottish, a 1982 Leyland Tiger TRCTL11/3R with Duple Goldliner body for the Edinburgh-London express service, at the company's Dryburgh Abbey Hotel when new in August.

Ensign has always been prepared to try something new, and at the Brighton Coach Rally in April 1982 exhibited this former London DMS-type Daimler Fleetline converted to left-hand drive and fitted with overseas requirements like full-depth sliding windows.

MILESTONES IN
DOUBLE-DECK BUS DESIGN

GAVIN BOOTH looks at an unlikely Milestone

Guy Arab Utility

Was there life before the Arab?

As we have seen, the double-decker had been in development since the early years of the 20th century, and by the end of the 1930s had reached a pretty sophisticated level, with diesel engines, often preselective gearboxes, and stylish bodywork. That all changed with the outbreak of war in 1939, and although what were essentially full prewar specification buses were still built for a while, the worsening war situation brought a sudden end to all bus production.

Buses clearly had an important part to play in the war effort, so a utility specification was drawn up that would allow the manufacture of no-frills buses as part of the war effort. Out went all the rounded panels, wood interior finishes and sumptuously-upholstered seats, and in came buses that simply shouted 'austerity'. Squared-off rear domes, the minimum number of opening windows, wooden-slatted seats and

a dull 'livery', often grey or brown, marked these out as basic no-nonsense buses.

At first it seemed that Leyland would become the main chassis supplier, but Leyland's factories were used for other war work and Bristol, Daimler and Guy found themselves building utility versions of their prewar double-deck chassis. Bristol was involved early in the war and came back towards the end; Daimler managed to keep production going in Wolverhampton after its Coventry works was bombed; but it fell to Guy to build the great majority of wartime double-deckers.

Although Guy had been around in bus and truck manufacture for some years, and had a double-deck chassis, the Arab, on its books since 1933, it was suddenly propelled into the front line of bus builders with orders for the utility Arab.

As delivered, utility Guy Arabs were uncompromising and rugged. These five Edinburgh Corporation Arab MkIs, some in fleet livery and others in grey, have bodywork by Massey (the bus in the centre) and Pickering. They are seen when new in 1943.

So, what was different about the Arab?

Actually, not a lot. The wartime bus was a reworking of its earlier chassis, which meant that it was rugged and straightforward with no concession to fashion. It had a Gardner engine, mostly the 7-litre 85bhp 5LW unit, though operators with hilly territory were often allowed to specify the 8.4-litre 102bhp 6LW. A constant mesh gearbox was fitted and brakes were servo-assisted. The wartime models were unofficially designated the Arab MkI and Arab MkII.

The bodywork was uncompromising and built by a wide range of companies, including mainstream firms like Park Royal and Weymann, as well as smaller firms like Massey and Northern Counties. Although the bodies were broadly similar in outline, they had individual quirks that helped recognition.

For operators desperate for buses the utility Arabs were a godsend, although the constant mesh gearboxes were not welcomed by drivers who had been used to preselective boxes, and often this led to their premature withdrawal once peace returned.

Where Guy went, did others follow?

In a way, yes. The utility Arab introduced Guys into many fleets that had previously standardised on the more mainstream types. After the war, when an

Restored to its former glory, London Transport G351, a 1945 Arab MkII with Park Royal body, is unveiled at Cobham Bus Museum in April 2005.
Gavin Booth

element of free choice returned, several operators continued to buy Guy models that were little different to the wartime version. Many engineers favoured the rugged, reliable and economical Gardner LW range of engines, and good wartime experiences led to postwar orders. In later years the Arab, which went through successive MkIII, MkIV and MkV forms, was supplied with Gardner's more powerful 6LX engine, and some operators chose preselective gearboxes and semi-automatic boxes.

The wartime body restrictions were gradually eased and what were essentially relaxed versions of the wartime bodies were supplied by several bodybuilders to help ease the postwar vehicle demand. And as Guy had benefited from its wartime exposure, some bodybuilders found themselves winning postwar orders on the strength of their wartime performance, notably Northern Counties, which broadened its customer base, no doubt partly because it was allowed to build all-metal bodies during the war while others struggled with unseasoned timber, which often led to premature withdrawal. **CB**

RALLYING THE CLASSICS

TONY WILSON looks at Those Magnificent Men (and Women) and their Driving Machines

IN A CONTRIBUTION WRITTEN BY DAVID Thrower in the 2006 edition of this tome, he asked the question 'Where Next for Bus Preservation?'. His fulsome text and final analysis made interesting reading and jogged me into riffling through my drawers(!) and pulling out a few reminders from rallies and events that I (sometimes accompanied by the memsahib and our daughter), attended up and down the country from the 1970s to the present date.

A couple we attended in the early years were the Godalming Gathering, that subsequently became the Southsea Spectacular and Brunelzebub, which developed into the massively successful Showbus many years later. These were initially very small beer, but by the time several years had passed were both much bigger, especially the latter which has probably become the largest such event of the rallying calendar (unless anyone disputes or knows better).

The Boss however, never fails on a regular basis to remind of the time we attended a one-off event in a disused coal yard at the back of King's Cross in the early 1970s. Wearing totally inappropriate clothing for the occasion (open-toed sandals and a light-coloured trouser suit – that was her by the way not me), what did she expect to emerge like at the end of the event, especially with the addition of the odd shower or three during the day? She learnt what to wear as the years progressed.

So sit back and enjoy a few untouched slides taken on my trusty non-digi 'heritage' camera, selected from my meagre collection taken over the years.

One can only hope that such an interest can be maintained for years to come, despite the ever-increasing amount of legislation being forced on the preservation movement by our political masters. **CB**

David opened his article making reference to the ex-General AEC Regal fleet number T31, so where better to start than with this vehicle seen here at one of the well-attended Cobham Bus Museum open days that for many, sees the start of the rallying season. The bus is seen near to the London Bus Preservation Group's (later Trust) premises just off the Redhill Road. Like many this event started from modest beginnings and has grown so much that the main focus for visiting vehicles has been on the nearby Wisley airfield for several years. A fleet of buses both young and old transport visitors between there and the museum's buildings on a network of services providing an opportunity to sample days gone by.

All photos by Tony Wilson

Above: It is to Brighton that we now travel and the annual Historic Commercial Vehicle Society's run down the main A23 trunk road from Battersea Park in London. Seen here arriving on to the seafront in May 1990 is this Tilling-Stevens TS7 with a Tilling 30-seat body. New to Thomas Tilling in 1925, the vehicle has for many years been looked after in the British Commercial Vehicle Museum at Leyland in Lancashire.

Below: Once in Brighton entrants were lined up on the seafront for inspection at Madeira Drive, where fleetnumber 139 in the Leeds City Transport fleet is observed. A 1934 AEC Regent supplied with a locally (to Leeds) built Roe body. Visitors to the event were able to cast their knowledgeable eyes over the vehicles on display from both ground level and above.

The Vintage Transport Association (ViTA) hosted a modest collection of preserved vehicles at Jordan's Garage at Godalming in April 1971. Advertised as the Godalming Gathering it was repeated the following year, but word spread and the group was invited to hold its 1973 event in the Portsmouth area. From then on it was established on the huge Common area at Southsea providing much variety for all who attended, judging by the large numbers of entries that turned up over the years. Arriving along the Esplanade in 1992 is Southdown no.772, a 1955 Leyland PD2 with Park Royal bodywork.

On several occasions during the 1980s and 1990s a bus rally was held in the grounds of the Netley Country Park, near to Southampton. Set in verdant surroundings on the shores of the Solent the park afforded an excellent backdrop for vehicles attending the event, none more so than the roadway on to the rally site. Heading a line of other vehicles entering the site in 1991 was no.63 in the pooled fleets of Brighton Corporation and Brighton Hove & District Transport, a 1939 AEC Regent with Weymann body.

'Go west young man' was the call. And so to Warminster and an event that was more than just a line-up of buses and coaches sat in a windswept field. This like a number of other such gatherings provided visitors the opportunity to ride around the surrounding countryside in various types and age of vehicle. This born and bred London author freely admits that his favourite double-decker is the Bristol K and not some red English capital city-based halfcab from the 1950s. Illustrating this statement that some may say was bordering on heresy, is no.353, a 1946 K6A from the Western National fleet sporting a fine lowbridge Eastern Coach Works body as it operates in service with passengers enjoying the experience.

Above: In the same area regular bus rallies have been held at several locations in and around the city of Bristol. August 1977 and buses are seen entering the site of one event held near the city centre to the obvious delight of the crowd. On this occasion a Crossley and a Dennis double-decker arrive beneath leaden skies. The Crossley, a 1949 DD42 model from Cardiff Corporation sports a crimson and cream-liveried Alexander body, whilst the nine years younger Dennis Loline in Aldershot & District colours has an East Lancs type in their pleasant well-known green and cream colours.

Below: We head northwards now into the West Midlands. The Kidderminster Rally usually held in the autumn was always a great pull for vehicle entries and visitors alike. Many of the vehicles would have had local operating connections but many others would have travelled to this popular event from far and wide to see vehicles such as this Weymann-bodied Daimler CVD6 built in 1950 and supplied to Exeter Corporation as its no.173.

Above: **Nottingham** has over the years been one of the regular locations for the annual AEC Rally. Here at the June 1994 event a double-decker in the shape of this 1939 AEC Renown with a Northern Counties body as no.329 in the Leicester City Transport fleet. The vehicle is currently housed at the Victorian Abbey Pumping Station museum in Leicester.

Below: One of the latest locations to add to the rally agenda is Chatsworth Park, home to the Duke and Duchess of Devonshire. Set in several thousand acres of the Peak District National Park, a bus rally was held for the first time during June 2006. Such was the success that a second helping was ordered for 2007. Almost 50 vintage buses and coaches attended, one such being this 1954 Daimler CVG6 with Weymann bodywork. Rotherham Corporation no.220 trundles gracefully along the family's private driveway, a concession granted for the day, as it heads for the rally site adjacent to the majestic setting of the house.

Left: In deepest West Yorkshire the town of Halifax has hosted a number of bus rallies over the years and as these events grew and drew ever-larger numbers of entrants so alternative sites were found. The rally in May 1994 included this Leyland Titan PD2 sporting a forward-entrance Massey body from 1966 and now owned by preservationists far from its origins in Lancashire, being housed in Bedfordshire. No.140 looks resplendent restored to full Wigan Corporation livery and displays a most interesting destination.

Below: Flying in the face of convention, this picture shows that one does not necessarily have to take a picture with the sun full out over the right shoulder. But of course it does depend on the subject matter and other considerations, as the shadows illustrate here. On the occasion of the annual open weekend event held by the Scottish Vintage Bus Museum at its Lathalmond base near Dunfermline in August 2003, these two double-deckers were on display in such a position as to make photography a little difficult when the sun was out. And as it spent the whole day beaming in a cloudless blue sky one was left with no alternative but to have a go. So here we have two former Edinburgh Corporation double-deckers, on the left a 1949 Daimler CVG6 alongside a 1954 Leyland Titan, both featuring Metro-Cammell bodywork.

Above: A small rally was held for many years in the coastal town of Dunbar. Situated at the mouth of the Firth of Forth the event included a road run, allowing visitors to ride on some of the vehicles and sample the delightful East Lothian countryside for around two hours. Regrettably circumstances saw the end of this rally some years ago, but not before this 1950 Albion Valiant CX39N type with a Duple 33-seat body passes along the town's High Street in August 1986. Whilst the vehicle is shown here sporting red/cream Western SMT livery, the vehicle came from Carmichael of Glenboig. Indeed the very editor of this illustrious tome was instrumental in the organisation of this event for many years.

Left: The Trolleybus Museum at Sandtoft is situated on the Isle of Axholme in North Lincolnshire. Home to one of the biggest collections of trolleybuses, regular open days are held throughout the year. In addition there has been an annual rally held here during July for a great many years. Representing a couple of the visiting vehicles over the years is first this 1965 East Lancs-bodied AEC Renown operated by Leicester City Transport arriving through the Isle of Axholme at the beginning of the day for the 2002 event. Turn back to page 54 for an earlier – and very different – Leicester Renown.

Above: A long way from its original home way down on the south coast is no.99 from the always-interesting Bournemouth Corporation trolleybus fleet. Now under the stewardship of the British Trolleybus Society this 1935 Park Royal-bodied Sunbeam is shown here at Sandtoft gently humming its way around the grounds and beneath the overhead in July 2003. The late Mike Dare must be remembered for his vision in the creation of this excellent collection of trolleybuses and memorabilia.

Below: Take a road due south from Sandtoft and you eventually reach Lincoln. Regular events are undertaken by members of the Lincolnshire Road Transport Museum at North Hykeham on the south side of the city and visitors are able to take rides around the local countryside on many of the vehicles that make the journey to the location and indeed others from within the collection. A fine line-up of an event in November 2002 saw these three parked together. From left to right number 23 in the Lincoln Corporation fleet a 1948 Guy Arab III, a Bristol MW from 1958 with Eastern Coachworks body number 2939 in the Bristol Omnibus fleet and FFU 860 a 1950 AEC Regal III with dual-purpose Willowbrook bodywork once with Enterprise of Scunthorpe.

Down at the bottom right-hand corner of East Anglia sits Southend-on-Sea. From a meeting with a similarly young couple and their children back in the very early 1970s, it transpired that they lived in this town and as our friendship grew over the years, so it became a regular event to meet up at least once a year. That this should coincide with the annual bus rally has no bearing whatsoever. Removes tongue from cheek and moves on. Held in Southchurch Park off Lifstan Way it was but a short walk from both the seafront and our host's home, where one could sample the delights such as this beautifully preserved 1956 Park Royal-bodied AEC Regent V formerly with Maidstone & District, as it enters the rally site in June 1993.

The annual North Weald rally was regrettably one that fell victim to increased pressures imposed upon organisers of such events. Held on the one-time wartime airfield adjacent to the M11 motorway in Essex, this was an ideal location for the rally, being out of the way of anyone who did not wish to be swept up in the comings and goings of the vehicles. Hard-standing on the wide-open runway concrete was excellent for vehicle display and on some occasions 'drive-a-bus' opportunities. However, inclement weather as sometimes happened meant the possibility of gale force winds coming direct from what seemed like the Urals, or blistering heat from beaming cloudless blue skies; mind you that can be the case for many such events up and down the country. Representing one of the successful years is this Jersey Motor Transport Leyland Titan approaches the rally site. Amongst others, Jim Blake was one of the prime movers behind this venture. As this is written, moves were afoot to reinstate the event for 2007.

Above: **What started as the brainchild of Martin Isles with a small gathering of buses at Brunel University, Uxbridge in what seems way back in the year dot, has as we all know metamorphosed into the annual Showbus Rally. It has become rather unkindly known throughout the bus world as 'Showerbus' for obvious reasons. However, it was not always like that. Much of the time yes, but not always, especially when one casts the mind back to some of those glorious weather days when the rally was held within the** confines of Woburn Park in Bedfordshire. Okay, so some of the vehicles had to be towed out by the resident tractor at the end of a dampish day. However, a reminder of one of those summer days is represented by this 1921 Leyland G7 with a Dodson 32-seater body. The vehicle had a relatively short distance to travel as it was entered by the great Leyland preservationist, Mike Sutcliffe, now honoured for his good works by being honoured with an MBE.

Right: **Our last picture takes us back to 1972 and the one-off rally held at glitzy King's Cross in London, already mentioned in the text. Conditions although far from perfect, did provide a hard-standing on ancient cobbles for the fair number of vehicles that attended the event. One entrant was this 1929 Leyland Titan TD1 that was new to National Omnibus & Transport, that sported Eastern Counties fleetname and livery on the day. If memory serves me right and according to the advert on the bus, the event was organised by the Historic Commercial Vehicle Club.**

THE COLOUR SUPPLEMENT

Colour shots that relate to articles elsewhere in this Yearbook

Above: MILESTONES IN DOUBLE-DECK BUS DESIGN
The impact that the Leyland Titan TD1 must have had on the bus industry in 1927 can be gauged from this view of the splendidly-restored 1928 Glasgow Corporation example that resides in the Scottish Vintage Bus Museum at Lathalmond, Fife.
Gavin Booth

Right: GOING MY WAY?
Geoff Burrows' all-time favourite destination layout, here on preserved Manchester Corporation no.2150, an all-Crossley DD42/8S dating from 1948.
Geoff Burrows

Above:
MILESTONES IN
DOUBLE-DECK
BUS DESIGN
Two examples of
the once-huge RT
family, brought
together in 1994
for a Classic Bus
head-to-head
roadtest –
RT2794 on the
left with the
Leyland
equivalent,
RTL1050.
Gavin Booth

Left: London
Country inherited
a fleet of RTs
from London
Transport that
were not entirely
suitable for some
of the work in
that area. RT3378
in Croydon in
July 1974.
Gavin Booth

Above: OLDHAM'S DISTINCTIVE FLEET A 1957 Oldham
Corporation Leyland PD2/20 with Roe body in the corporation's
distinctive pommard and Devon cream colours, in Oldham in
August 1974 after the undertaking had become part of Selnec PTE,
hence the vinyl.
Gavin Booth

Below: One of the four Leyland Tiger Cub PSUC1/3 with Marshall
41-seat two-door bodies makes heavy weather of the long climb
into Oldham town centre in August 1974, by which time it had
received Selnec livery.
Gavin Booth

Above: THE SECONDHAND TROLLEYBUS BOOM In 1961
Reading took delivery of its last trolleybuses, 12 Sunbeam F4A
with Burlingham 68-seat bodies, and five were sold to Teesside
Municipal Transport, including no.192 seen in Reading.
Michael Dryhurst

Below: MILESTONES IN DOUBLE-DECK BUS DESIGN
Now preserved, two of the first production Leyland Atlanteans –
both had been 1958 Commercial Motor Show exhibits –
came together at an open day at Clydeside's Greenock depot.
Wallasey Corporation no.1 has Metro-Cammell bodywork
and Glasgow Corporation LA1 has an Alexander body.
Gavin Booth

HAPPY ANNIVERSARY...

ROBERT E. JOWITT celebrates – along with various other noteworthy dates and the habitual repetitions and deviations – 35 years of writing for 'Buses Annual', 'Buses Yearbook', and, of course, in more recent times, 'Classic Bus Yearbook'

IT IS 50 YEARS AGO TODAY, AS I WRITE THESE words, that I first fell in love. On 26 June 1956 Gianna Conte of Genoa, Italy, and her retinue, stepped off a Hants & Dorset bus at Paddy's Gap, Milford-on-Sea, Hants. (I might here perhaps usefully explain that this was the nearest bus stop to the Jowitt family holiday residence.)

I have no means of ascertaining, half a century later,

As one of his earlier artistic endeavours Jowitt always considered this view of a 1950 Bournemouth BUT trolleybus in a Pokesdown tavern window rather a fine study, but so far as he can recall no editor has yet shared this view; perhaps this will now change.

Photos by Robert E Jowitt, excepted where indicated

CITY

97

Early Jowitt classic; four different sorts of trams in Sheffield in 1959. Buses, deemed boring, conspicuous by their absence!

what sort of bus it was, but suspect it to have been an ECW lowbridge Bristol K6A or similar, there being many of these on the routes between Bournemouth and Lymington. As for the retinue (as I must deem it in face of the fact that Gianna's presence fast dwarfed for me the rest of the party) it consisted of her sister Chicca – about 15, I think, a year older than Gianna or me – and their mother (a reputed gynaecologist, I believe) and a Scottish widow (not the sexy black-scarfed type of the adverts in recent years but an eminently sensible and well-read lady, a dear friend of my mother's) and her sister, a fey lady who wandered round Europe picking up sundry acquaintance, hence the Conte presence at her sister's dwelling in Bournemouth.

I played records to the girls, 78s on a wind-up HMV, 'Zambezi' by Lou Busch, 'The Ballad of Davy Crockett', Tennessee Ernie Ford, or 'Only You' and 'The Great Pretender' by the Platters; and they loved them, but as I play the original discs again today they sound as archaic as the roar of a K6A.

A few days ago, having occasion to visit Lymington, I paid a sentimental journey to Paddy's Gap. Who Paddy was I had never discovered. His gap, a chine sufficient in 1940 to be barricaded with five large concrete blocks, was sufficiently eroded that by 1956 the blocks were tumbled on the beach and the Conte girls and I could

build sandcastles on them. Now, in 2006, there was nothing left of gap or blocks, the tumbling cliffs had been stabilised by an ugly sea-wall, and all the Victorian villas along the cliff-top had been razed to make way for blocks of shoe-box flats. A scene all but unrecognisable. One or other of the two bus shelters looked as if it might have survived from the day Gianna arrived and departed, but I couldn't be sure...

The fey Scots lady brought them over again the next day, K6A and 'Zambezi' again, and the girls in the same blue cotton jeans with red turn-ups just below the knee and horizontally thin-striped T-shirts in white and blue. Gianna was brown-eyed and black-haired. Two days later I collected Gianna and Chicca from the Scottish widow's house in Christchurch Road, we descended to Bournemouth Square on a 1936 Sunbeam trolleybus and proceeded thence to Sandbanks on one of those famous H&D flat-front open-top 1952/53 rebuilds of earlier K6As or whatever. We crossed on the chain ferry, strayed along Shell Bay beach with me falling ever more in love, and then returned to Christchurch Road via ferry, H&D, and BCT trolleybus as before.

Jowitt album pages, c1960-62, of portraits of Bournemouth belles, including several of the surviving 1935 Sunbeam trolleybuses ... and Carol.

Above: **The type of bus on which the author travelled to take young ladies to the family home for respectable tea. King Alfred FOT 771, Reading-bodied Leyland Tiger PS1/1 of 1947, turning round, with difficulty, in the Jewry Street car park on a short-working in 1959 near the end of its existence.**

Right: **French trolleybuses were always desirable, but the new trams in St Etienne in 1960 seemed at the time too blandly modem.** *Si jeunesse savait . . .* **The advertisements on the buildings were still fairly typical at that date, but dying fast.**

Above: **Old France, Quimper, Brittany, 1967.** Rear views of three classic (rounded-front) Chaussons, while the fourth, unidentified, boasts thoroughly French spare wheel and luggage rack. The lady's Sunday headgear is (or was) fairly normal in that district.

Left: **Girls eating ice-creams/1.** When Jowitt was first writing for 'Buses Annual' Lodekkas and the like were still common enough; this one, with Crosville, was actually in Chester some 10 or a dozen years earlier.

I saw Gianna once again, a year later, (at Frensham Pond near Farnham, actually) at which juncture she chose to decry my protestations of eternal love – which I had already committed to letters and now repeated verbally – as *scioccio*. I do not recall if I ever checked the exact translation in an Italian dictionary, it was obvious enough... but 50 years later I still recall, as every year since the first, the day of Gianna.

Magic number

What, however, does the apparently magic number 50 really represent? Why not 49 or 51? While I walked beside my first love on the beach of Milford-on-Sea the 50th anniversary of the introduction of regular motorbus services in Paris, 16 June 1906 with Brillie-Schneider double-deckers was but a few days past, little as I recked of it then, though it had influence

enough in my life thereafter. Now, as I write, it must therefore obviously be the centenary. Any number can be significant. Why 21 for your child (traditionally) when you have already let it loose (legally) at 18?

Let us therefore attend on the number 35. 35 years, the period, seems to have become established, in the English mentality, as some kind of joke, like bloomers or mothers-in-law, the stuff of pantomime or Bamforth postcards. Perhaps its origin derived from lines in the 'Goon Show' or 'Beyond the Fringe'. A few years later the same occurred with the Beatles' words on 'When I'm 64' living in a cottage in the Isle of Wight. To this last accusation I must admit that I am at present guilty.

Anyway, 35 years ago, my first submitted – and indeed requested – article appeared in 'Buses Annual', then lately taken under the editorial wing of Gavin Booth. Probably a number of readers who study these words now were not then even born; those who were may spare a wry smile. Now of course in dealing with an issue (please pardon the pun, if you deem it so to be) such as 'Buses Annual' the matter of actual dates is very much less clear-cut than that of falling in love.

Left: **Girls eating ice-creams/2.** When Jowitt was first writing for 'Buses Annual' Leyland Nationals were a novelty; this one, starting life with Hants & Dorset, is seen a dozen or so years later in Hampshire Bus guise, in Winchester St George Street.

Below: **Leyland Nationals poured in throughout the 1970s,** not necessarily desirable in the author's eyes. This Midland Red example is in Birmingham. Not sure about the ultimate desirability of two different coloured legs, either.

The 'Buses Annual' in question was entitled simply 'Buses Annual'... on the cover, though the title page grants us 'Buses Annual 1972', but was published in 1971, so we may assume that I was actually writing for it 35 years ago.

Now here you, the reader, may reasonably cry 'Hang on, I am not reading 'Buses Annual' or even 'Buses Yearbook' (by which title, in more recent years, the invaluable work has come to be known); no, I am reading 'Classic Bus Yearbook'.' You must recall, then, that for many years Gavin Booth was Editor of 'Buses Annual' and later 'Buses Yearbook', before handing over the editorial mantle to the equally competent Stewart Brown and branching out into *Classic Bus*, the magazine, and, of course, 'Classic Bus Yearbook'. To this possibly complex tale I can add only that as Gavin Booth encouraged me at the first in my vices of verboseness and untoward attitudes in bus photography – not but what Stewart Brown seemed eager enough to keep me on his list – I felt that it should fall to Gavin to receive the first fruits of meditation on 35 years. Nevertheless, following a tri-partite conference, it was agreed that these 35 years should be celebrated also in the real 'Buses Yearbook', so that to anything I may say in these, the pages of 'Classic Bus Yearbook', there will be appended, when, slightly later it appears, further comments on the subject of 35 years in 'Buses Yearbook 2008'. To which I hasten to add that, like in any series of Enid Blyton stories, the characters will be the same but each piece or offering will be entire in itself. Naturally, however, it is my hope, and that of both the editors, that the devoted reader will gladly suffer these slightly unusual circumstances and acquire both volumes!

Before I proceed further into the topics of which I was writing 35 years ago I must crave from the reader a little more tolerance on the subject of anniversaries.

I am ever conscious of the lugubrious percipience of Tess (of the d'Urbervilles – Thomas Hardy) in reflecting that some date in the calendar of life – a date like a birthday but of course unknown – must mark the date of death. There must come a time when I write no more

for 'Buses-whatever'. It could well be argued that having done it for 35 years this might be the moment to say 'enough' but I remember the tale of the last steam train to Exeter – now, 40 years ago, another anniversary! – which, having been steamed and run once, was steamed and run again several times more (though I forget how many). Shall I not do likewise!

Why?

Here, however, the eternal question: why write or photograph for 'Buses Annual' at all? Well, people have always liked portraying travel with prose, poetry or picture; the Romans illustrated chariots, for example, on pots and pavements, and our 18th century forbears loved to capture the romance of stagecoaches, soon to be overtaken in reality and in art by the railways. In the course of time the charm of railway photography was added to the catalogue. In the end there followed the tram and the bus, even if more humble in mien.

The purist – or nit-picker – may proclaim that at this moment I am not writing about buses. Verily I am not. I am – read this carefully – writing about writing about buses. Quite as important a task!

It so happened that in my youth I took scant interested in buses, except when they conveyed me and a girl, as in the case of Sandbanks and Gianna or, a bit later, King Alfred single deckers transporting me and a certain Mary from the centre of Winchester to my home on the northern outskirts. My early photographs were of trams – German or English – and trolleybuses which boasted an allure lacking in ordinary buses. My first tram photograph was in Paderborn, Germany, 1958, another 50th anniversary coming up! But I have written of this before, and even if repetition is the prerogative of the senile – as may be proven in these passages – I do not know how far I dare push my luck! To return to the original topic, or my lack of interest in

Top: **Trolleybuses were always meritorious, as witness fine three-axle vehicle of unknown make in not entirely elegant surroundings in Genoa, Italy in 1966.**

Above: **The last days of the 1936 Renault TN4H in Paris in 1970. Jowitt (right) soon to start writing (first of all on French buses) for 'Buses Annual', appears to overshadow by several inches driver Emile Hammes and conductor Touitou Leopold, but it should be noted they are standing in the gutter and he on the pavement.**

buses: I made exception for certain very elderly buses, especially those passed on to fairground use, and a few continental oddities such as articulated buses or the latest German half-deckers. If some of this work was simply 'record-shots' I was soon indulging in frontal and broadside portraits as well – I am not sure in what category to include my efforts at catching as many as I

could of the fast vanishing Bournemouth 1935 Sunbeams full-face – and including architecture and humans and especially the girls for which I have since, for better or worse, become famous. All this was accompanied by exuberant traveller's tales in my diary.

The emphasis changed in France in 1960 where, though trolleybuses abounded, so far as trams were concerned I encountered only the blandly modernised single route of St Etienne (though choice enough its cars seemed when I saw them again 29 years later!) but the buses made up for this, being in great degree possessed of a Gallic charm – albeit with a tendency to 'juke-box' fronts – and character not to be found anywhere else. This distinction applied above all to the buses of Paris, a large proportion of the fleet at that date consisting of the celebrated open-rear-platform Renault TN of the 1930s, many of a style two decades out of date when they were new! Now here again the question of repetition risks raising its head. My love-affair with and eventual purchase of certain Renault TN buses – it took 10 years from the birth of the idea to its first fruits of achievement – has often been told.

Oh Carol!

Before this happy day I was busy pursuing trams and trolleybuses … and light railways … here and there in western Europe, sometimes with my first true girlfriend Carol of Bournemouth who has thus often featured in these pages, so here again no more repetition! My first published photograph – in the *Hampshire Chronicle* – was however a British Railways steam train, one of the last workings of the railway from Brockenhurst to Ringwood, Hants, and on into Dorset, May 1964. Viennese trams with a flowery text (despite some editorial deletions!) followed in the late-lamented *Old Motor* magazine, plus, for example, steam trains on the Isle of Wight in *Hampshire Magazine*. The breakthrough came with Ian Allan's publishing of 'A Desire of Tramcars' in 1969 with a companion volume 'A Silence of Trolleybuses' a couple of years later. Both volumes were based on the precept of assembling the vehicles in the categories of their surroundings rather than by system or make or

Above left: **The new look in the early 1970s – not then entirely to Jowitt's liking with curvaceous windscreen, but now of course a treasure – King Alfred Metro Scania AOU 110J.**

Above: **Jowitt always considered it just as vital a part of bus photography to include passengers (or perhaps just people waiting to cross the road) as it was to include the bus – or just a detail of the bus, here the open rear platform of a Paris 1936 Renault TN4H.**

type, so you had 'trams (or trolleybuses) and towers and spires' or 'trams and birds and beasts' – this latter title, please note, referred to hens and pigeons, though there was also a section on 'trams and girls'. It seems now a pity that I never completed the trilogy with 'A Bellowing of Buses', for even then I could have scraped together sufficient buses to make a worthwhile volume, and though I have offered the notion here and there in more recent times it remains a dream. Part of the problem back then was that I was deeply engaged in my epic 'Paris is Well Worth a Bus' (published by Jersey Artists in January 1971 to coincide with the last Renault TN services) which perforce creamed off the chief gems in the potential collection, and I couldn't do two books including Paris simultaneously. Well, actually I could, easily, but . . .

Such works were not entirely well-received in certain quarters, and I must admit that I had undertaken them partly in the hopes of shocking the more hidebound

section of the transport enthusiast old guard, one or two of whom, I felt, considered me a cocky young revolutionary. I suppose I am bound to admit that I was a fairly arrogant youth. On the other hand the renowned transport author Ian Yearsley described 'A Desire of Tramcars' as 'a new dimension in tramway literature' and, even if the editor of *Buses Illustrated* spoke somewhat scathingly of certain aspects of 'A Silence of Trolleybuses', evidently Gavin Booth was sufficiently bold to risk adding me to his new charge. Moreover, even though xenophobia was rife among British bus enthusiasts in those days, he requested I write about French Buses. So I did.

100,000 words

Since then, including that first 'L'Autobus' I have written – I think – 31 pieces for 'Buses Annual/Yearbook' – and eight for 'Classic Bus Yearbook', to which add two more if you count the present and forthcoming efforts. This amounts, at the very least, to something like 100,000 words – or the length, approximately, of an earlyish Jilly Cooper girlie-novel – and with at least 300 photographs. It is my hope, in the companion pages to this volume, to make some review of the various subjects upon which I have touched and some mention of changes to the scenes I surveyed.

As for the few issues for which I was absent... well, one or two numbers are missing from my shelves, due to my parsimonious habit of waiting to buy a copy until they became cheaper at next year's flea-markets, and then not finding one, so for all I know there may be one or two contributions which have escaped my memory entirely. Another miss was a deliberate (and to my way of thinking extremely ill-conceived) decision by the publishers not to include a Jowitt piece; as a consequence of which in a fit of pique I went ahead and published 'The Girl in the Street' which, in a large review, was described as 'by some way the oddest book the *Sunday Times* has ever received . .' There was another large review in the Dutch newspaper *Handelsblad* which said, I guess, much the same. Another exclusion from the pages came about by editorial double-booking, and I effectively lost the toss but as I have great sympathy for such human frailty I forgave him. Why I was missing on the other occasions I have no idea; perhaps my own frailty caused me to forget to remind the editors that they might like me to make a contribution. Or there is, of course, the remote possibility, low be it spoken, that my editors, be they never so broad-minded, felt that the anti-clan needed a break from high Edwardian phraseology with clauses and sub-clauses making a sentence last nearly half a page along with maiden-besplattered impressionist photography!

Of the list of contributors in 1972, only three names occur again in Buses 2007, those being Gavin Booth, Stewart J. Brown ... and Robert E. Jowitt. It is possibly of some interest to note that in the subsequent three-and-a-half decades Robert E. Jowitt, first in one house and then in another in Winchester, moved on to Herefordshire and eventually to the Isle of Wight, while Stewart Brown (actually, I believe, a Glaswegian) moved from Lancashire to Gloucestershire and back to Lancashire and Gavin Booth remained steadfastly in

the same address in Edinburgh. So far as I am concerned my peregrinations have had some influence on my contributions. I cannot speak for Messrs Booth and Brown.

The two dozen or so articles in the earlier issues are new reduced by roughly half, the number of pages is approximately the same, therefore the articles must be longer! The cover price in 1972 was £1.50, in the then nearly new decimal coinage which was to bring about that rollicking inflation resulting in the book now costing tenfold! The standard of paper has improved, and colour, starting with four sides, now fills almost the entire 'Buses Yearbook'. (Note here that 'Buses Yearbook' commenced its new title as 'Buses Year Book', transmogrified in 1994). 'Classic Bus Yearbook', by the nature and date of its subject matter, still retains a fair percentage of black-and-white. But I must admit to regarding it a pity that two colour pictures of mine of Teme Valley Duple Dominants in lurid new livery or with golden autumn leaves managed

Top: **Foreign travels were always an inspiration for Jowitt essays. Halcyon days in the 1960s on the lake of Thun, Switzerland, with the paddle-steamer Blümlisalp (1906?) and a sleepy trolleybus and trailer.**

Above: **Jowitt dislike of buses in general in the late 1950s/early 1960s never included more obscure continental specimens, as witness this splendid Vienna three-axle double-decker seen in 1963. Nonetheless this shot somehow missed inclusion in the 1973 article of 'Seats on Top in Several Languages'.**

to escape into the black-and-white pages while to make matters worse the tops of the golden trees had been editorially lopped, sadly prophetic as the trees have in reality now been felled. It might have been kind of Mr Booth to include them here again in glorious technicolor but in the intervening period Jowitt has naturally enough lost the prints!

Lopping or not we may note that quite a quantity of buses now estimated as 'classic' first took the roads in

an era when black-and-white photography was starting to wane and colour was becoming affordable and popular. Furthermore many buses now counted among the elect had not then seen the light of day, or only just! Leyland Nationals and Bristol VRs were in their infancy. That which seemed ordinary then, like Lodekkas, has been transformed into desirable, that which was new and to the traditionalist ugly has mellowed into grace. A whole generation of buses has come ... and, nearly, gone! This is a sobering thought; 35 years is in very truth an uncommon long time.

It is incidentally an excessive long time in which to attempt to preserve a bus that was 35 years old when you began the caper – in other words to double its lifespan – as I know to my cost. It becomes increasingly impossible to face decay which was already in evidence when they were running on borrowed time in Paris ... unless you are a millionaire with large well-equipped workshop, plenty of labour, and possessed of boundless energy. None of this applies to me now, much of it never did, but I had wonderful times with my veterans and the crews who volunteered for them, sometimes for a second almost recreating what it had been like in Paris. No preservation can truly achieve, however, what the mood was like, nor bus nor tram nor train; there is always a degree of self-consciousness in the effort. Furthermore, when the present generation that remembers is gone, how will the rising generation view these relics? Perhaps as any of us view dinosaur skeletons ... Acquaintances of mine have brought French exchange students to look at my buses in the belief that, as French, they would prove of interest, and these young people have gaped at them completely uncomprehendingly, and without much enthusiasm at that. Boring! There can be little doubt that many buses now in preservation will become, when those who first saved them are no longer there to strive and to care, especially in an increasingly hostile and litigating bureaucratic environment, little better than skeletons. If that . . .

Is it thoughts like these, even if deep in the subconscious, which make some of us take photographs of buses and write about travel? An attempt to capture a vanishing world. Even had Renault TNs, for example, or likewise Routemasters, hung on longer than they did, in a changing society they must soon have developed into anachronisms as self-conscious as ... oh, for example, brewers' drays!

Morbid lines

The reader may have perused, in recent pages of bus literature, perhaps even in previous issues of this Yearbook, morbid lines in the same vein as those immediately here above, but penned by other authors than this. Do not suppose, however, that I am simply imitating them, even if I echo them; such notions have been in my head – and increasingly – for quite a while. In the end, however, whatever befalls the buses themselves, we may be fairly sure that the memories will remain on the printed page at least; and now and then perhaps someone will mark an anniversary, even for some event they cannot possibly remember. No one, of course, will recall 26 June 1956. I very much doubt that it is remembered by Gianna Conte herself.

(Post-script. Some six months after I started this article, and – with editorial fire now breathing furiously about deadlines, but before readers start lavishing upon me a sympathy which possibly I do not merit – though any sympathy is always balm to a starving author – I may usefully add that at the Winchester Running Day on 1 January 2007 I managed to acquire, at very reasonable price, on a stall manned – or in this case, actually, girled – by my own dear Friends of King Alfred Buses, most of the numbers hitherto missing from my shelves; these issues, while packed with fascinating material from Messrs Brown and Booth and several other notable contributors, proved in fact not to boast any missing Jowitt jewels. At least it makes the shelves look tidier!) CB

OLDHAM'S DISTINCTIVE FLEET

DAVID WAYMAN describes the Oldham bus fleet from 1944 to the formation of Selnec PTE

OLDHAM HAS ALWAYS BEEN PUNISHING territory for buses. The very name of the place is probably derived from Auld Hulme or Aldholm, meaning 'elevated meadowland' or 'promontory'. Its hills are the Pennines of course, and much of the town centre is practically 700ft above sea level, approached by relatively steep or long climbs or undulations on all sides. North-east of the centre, within in four miles the 1,100ft contour is reached at the exposed settlement of Grains Bar on the A672 road.

At the end of World War 2, Oldham Corporation Passenger Transport Department had a fleet of 214 buses, predominantly 1930s Leyland Titans of types TD3, TD4 and TD5 (plus 27 trams, which would be gone within 15 months). As it was well-stocked early in the war OCPTD had no need of utility buses. The prewar order for 47 Leyland TD5s (nos.180-226) had anticipated the abolition of the two remaining tram routes, but due to the need to conserve imported fuels the Ministry of Transport would not sanction the withdrawal in late 1939

of the Manchester-Oldham-Waterhead tram service, operated jointly with Manchester Corporation. Accordingly sufficient trams were retained, which meant that Oldham was in the fortunate position of having a surplus of buses and able to hire some out during the war. However, the cross-suburban Hollinwood-Shaw tram route required extensive track renewal and so authority was granted for its withdrawal on 2 December 1939 with the substitution of buses.

Oldham did acquire three buses during the war, however. Early in 1944 with the Manchester and Rochdale municipal undertakings it purchased Yelloway Motor Services' limited-stop service between Rochdale and Manchester. As part of the transaction an all-Leyland Titan TD5 joined the Oldham fleet, along with two Burlingham-bodied petrol-engined Tiger TS1 coaches that were immediately sold on. Then during 1946-49 an assortment of 110 new buses joined the fleet, all except ten of them double-deckers. Here are details of 1944-49 acquisitions.

1946 Roe-bodied Leyland Titan PD1 No228, Oldham's numerically first postwar bus, is seen here hurrying eastwards across Star Inn Junction, homebound and showing service letter 'X' denoting depot or other irregular working.

1944

227 (DDK 256) Leyland TD5/Leyland H30/26R w/d 1952 (Ex-Yelloway, new 1938)

(DK 7378/9) Leyland TS1/Burlingham C29R w/d 1944 (Ex-Yelloway, not operated)

1946

228-41 (DBU 20-33) Leyland PD1/Roe H31/25R w/d 1966/7

The following and all future new buses were 8ft wide and where registration numbers match fleetnumbers, only registration letters are given

1947/48

242-91 (DBU) Leyland PD1/3/Roe H31/25R w/d 1966-8

1948

292-301 (DBU) Crossley SD42/3/Roe B32F we/d 1961-8

302-11 (EBU 465-74) Crossley DD42/5/Crossley H30/26R w/d 1963-5

312-21 (EBU 912-21) Daimler CVD6/Roe H31/25R w/d 1965/6

1949

322-36 (EBU 922-36) Daimler CVD6/Crossley H30/26R w/d 1966

1948

337 (EBU 867) Leyland PD2/3/Roe H31/25R w/d 1966

The Titan PD1 was the immediate postwar Leyland double-deck model, although only an interim type until the larger-engined Titan PD2 was properly developed. Leyland's new constant-mesh gearbox as fitted to the PD1 was 'unforgiving'. Upward ratio-changes were normally slow which of course on Oldham's terrain affected performance adversely. This situation was not helped by the difficulty in mastering the technique of using the clutch-stop for faster changes. Although the 7.4-litre engine had a rating of 100bhp @ 1,800rpm, on some of Oldham's climbs it was hard-pressed. In contrast to the prewar Leyland diesel it emitted a harsh knock, heard but fortunately not felt.

The Roe bodies of the PD1s were not fitted with saloon heaters and their seats were upholstered in leathercloth rather than the more usual moquette. Crews called these buses 'utilities' but in fact they were not, as that colloquialism applied only to buses built to the national 'standard wartime specification'. Although having been ordered during the 'utility' period when operators had to apply for a licence to purchase buses, these examples were of Roe's postwar outline and construction. They introduced a revised Oldham characteristic: an additional service number indicator in place of the offside destination indicator.

In 1941 there had been a raising of the maximum gross weight for psvs from 10.5 tons to 11 tons, and then in 1946 to 12 tons with an increase of maximum width to 8ft. From 1947, the year in which Park Royal Vehicles acquired Chas H. Roe, Oldham standardised on a width of 8ft and the Leyland designation PD1/3 denoted the difference. The PD1/3s were delivered in two batches of 25, the later batch not having the 'proud' waistrails that normally characterised Roe bodies. However all were fully up to prewar levels of comfort with moquette-covered seats and saloon heaters, again to be standard.

The chassis designation of 302-11 is puzzling as Crossley lists normally stated that the DD42/5 model was 7ft 6in wide and the DD42/4 8ft. However, although nos.302-11 certainly were 8ft wide, Oldham internal documents clearly state DD42/5. The Crossley constant-mesh gearbox had faster upward changes was easier to handle than the Leyland unit. Crossley, having recently moved from Gorton in Manchester to Stockport, was acquired by AEC in 1948, as was Maudslay. Along with the bodywork concerns Park Royal, which already included Roe, and Crossley coachworks, the large new organisation soon became known as Associated Commercial Vehicles, vying with Leyland for supremacy in the bus and commercial vehicle markets. As to the

The 8ft width of the Titan PD1/3 may be detected here as no.252 picks up in Union Street.

R H G Simpson

still owned on 1 November 1969 were to pass into the ownership of the Selnec PTE and those surviving after 1 April 1974 to that of the Greater Manchester PTE.

1950

338-51 (EBU 868-81) Leyland PD2/3/Roe H31/25R w/d 1968-70

352-61 (FBU 639-48) Leyland PD2/3/Roe H31/25R w/d 1968-70

362-5 (FBU 821-4) Crossley SD42/7/Roe B32F w/d 1965-7

366-9 (FBU 825-8) Crossley DD42/8/Crossley H30/26R w/d 1966-8

1952

370-2 (HBU 123-5) Leyland PD2/12/Leyland H30/26R w/d 1968-70

Daimlers, they had the standard preselector gearbox and Daimler's CD6-type engine, introduced 1945 and a highly refined unit among diesels. Crossley coachworks were to have bodied the whole 25 but due to uncertain delivery dates an order for 10 of the bodies was switched to Roe.

The PD2/3 was the first 8ft-wide version of the range and Oldham no.337, lacking an offside service number indicator, was a Roe exhibit at the 1948 Commercial Motor Exhibition in London. The other 24 of the batch were not delivered until 1950. With their brawny 9.8-litre engine of the new O.600 type and synchromesh on second to fourth gear ratios they could make lighter work of Oldham's fearsome gradients than most other types.

Here are details of these vehicles and others delivered 1950-52. It should be noted that all vehicles

The eight Crossleys, nos.362-9, had the HOE7/5 'downdraught' type of engine, which was found to be somewhat more efficient than the earlier 'HOE' types. It had a pleasant tone that blended agreeably with the high-pitched whine of the synchromesh gearbox. The trio of PD2/12s were of the new 27ft length, permissible from 1950, showing the Leyland body in its final development, still well-proportioned and restrained in appearance.

Yet another era was about to begin, one where the traditional exposed radiator was no longer to be seen but concealed on new vehicles joining the Oldham fleet. The style, which other chassis manufacturers offered too, was described as the 'new look' or 'tin front'. The Leyland example may not have been the most tasteful, being a somewhat bulbous creation based on what Leyland had already produced for the large Midland Red company; the 'concealed radiator' style of front was usually optional and by no means all operators were to specify it. Oldham's 'tin-front Titans' are listed here. Nos.388-462 did not have synchromesh mechanism on second ratio.

1955

373-7 (KBU 383-7) Leyland PD2/20/Met-Cam H30/26R w/d 1970/1

1954

378-87 (KBU 373-82) Leyland PD2/20/Roe H31/25R w/d 1973

1957

388-407 (NBU 488-507) Leyland PD2/20/Roe H33/27R w/d by 1974

408-12 (NBU 508-12) Leyland PD2/20/Crossley H33/28R w/d 1970/73

413-8 (NBU 513-8) Leyland PD2/20/NCME H33/28R w/d 1974/5

1958/59

419-28 (PBU 919-28) Leyland PD2/30/Met-Cam H37/28R 1971-5

1958

429-52 (PBU 929-52) Leyland PD2/30/Roe H37/28R w/d 1973-5

1958/59

453-62 (PBU 953-62) Leyland PD2/30/NCME H33/28R w/d 1970-4

During the early and mid 1950s there was also a trend nationally towards lighter buses. While some double-deckers were truly lightweight at less than seven tons unladen as in prewar years, only the numerically first small batch of Oldham's 'tin-front Titans' came near that figure. Their bodies were

ordered only after a delegation from the cautious Oldham Transport Committee had visited the Metro-Cammell works to examine how that concern's lightweight Orion-type bodywork was being built. Metropolitan-Cammell-Weymann Ltd (MCW), the marketing organisation for the Metropolitan-Cammell Carriage & Wagon Co of Birmingham and Weymanns Ltd of Addlestone, Surrey, held the patents for the Orion design and others.

Unpopular with crews and passengers, Oldham's five Orion-bodied Titans (nos.373-7) tended to bounce harshly on anything but the smoothest of road surfaces, especially when lightly loaded. Crews referred to them as 'loaf tins'. They were cold in winter and hot in summer. Much of the weight saved was at the expense of amenity as for example with the bare-looking frameless single-skin roof domes at front and

Above: **The Roe bodywork on the Titan PD2/3s differed only in minor detail from that fitted to the PD1/3s, as illustrated by no.356 in Yorkshire Street.**
R H G Simpson

Left: **Ah now, the DD42/8 was a Crossley to be reckoned with! Lovely smooth downdraught engine with a resonant tone and adequate power: it's just a pity that was so late in evolving. No.368, with the usual and distinctive Crossley body features, and seen in Greaves Street, is preserved.**
John Fozard

construction with teak framing, although in the case of nos.388-407 and 429-52 the timber was confined to the lower saloon, the upper being aluminium alloy-framed.

A further trend of the period was to increase seating capacities. Double-deckers from the late 1930s and up to no.387 had been 56-seaters. The 1957 Roe-bodied batch (nos.388-407) had 60 seats and the Crossley (nos.408-12) and Northern Counties (nos.413-8) batches 61. However, the 1958/59 batches (nos.419-62) all had 65 seats, the highest total achievable in a 27ft-long double-decker without fitting

rear. The Leyland 'tin front' was of the same width as for an 8ft-wide chassis as for a 7ft 6in-wide one and therefore in the case of the former it was necessary in plan view to taper-in the body front to match up. With the Orion front dome this created a particularly gaunt appearance. But Orion-bodied Titans! There are two Greek references there and perhaps one of them should have been another: Spartan! The second batch of Orion bodies (on nos.419-28) were of somewhat better specification and 14cwt heavier unladen, with better riding characteristics.

The Roe-bodied batches (nos.378-87, 388-407 and 429-52), while incorporating some lightweight materials, were substantially built and only marginally lighter than the heaviest PD2s (nos.337-61). All had the characteristically handsome appearance of Roe bodies and were of that concern's legendary composite

a rearward-facing quintuple bench seat at the front of the lower saloon. In the case of Roe bodies, the fitting of more than 33 seats in the upper saloon could not be achieved without altering the double-landing 'safety' staircase from the '2-5-1' design to '3-4-1'.

Crossley body designs by this period had lost their individuality and were to Park Royal design, but nonetheless attractive and well proportioned. Oldham's examples (nos.408-12), however, did not turn out to be as durable as some bodies of other makes and indeed earlier Crossley products. In later years the body of no.409 received extensive remedial treatment but it was not considered economic to extend this to the other four and they were withdrawn before any other NBU-registered examples. Wigan-based Northern Counties Motor & Engineering Co (NCME) had acquired a reputation for soundly built, robust and well-proportioned bodywork. Oldham took two relatively small batches (nos.413-8, 453-62).

The last of the prewar Leylands was withdrawn in 1958, except for one, no.205, which was deroofed shortly before its planned withdrawal date. Rather than scrapping it, the corporation converted it to a breakdown tender in which role it served for a further decade wearing an all-crimson lake livery and was known to crews as Red Biddy.

Following the 1959 deliveries five years elapsed without any new buses being acquired. However, it was a time of decision-making as to future double-decker policy: to persist with forward-engined types or to switch to rear-engined, a type that was gaining national popularity? The maximum length for two-axle double-deckers had been increased to 30ft in 1956 and by 1960 there were two makes of rear-engined chassis of that length on the market, their bodywork usually capable of housing up to 78 seats. After hiring several vehicles for evaluation Oldham bought further Leyland double-deck models, initially some Titan PD3s and then Atlantean PDR variations. For single-deck needs, Leyland Tiger Cub PSUC and Panther Cub PSRC types followed by Panther PSUR types were acquired. Here is the list, all Leylands and all 30ft long unless stated otherwise and with matching registrations; italics indicate reversed registrations, eg 101 JBU. The final two batches were not delivered until after the formation of the Selnec PTE on 1 November 1969.

Left: **No.410** here exhibits its Crossley body of Park Royal outline, in a style obviously derived from that being developed for the London Routemaster. The beautifying effect of the vermilion lining-out may be seen, although it was subsequently to be omitted for economy of repainting.

Below: **The 65-seat Roe bodies, with their modified stairs, had no staircase window as no.433 shows** while on test high up at the bleak Grains Bar. The road sign (left) denotes the Lancashire/West Riding of Yorkshire boundary.

1964
101-10 (HBU) PD3/5/Roe H41/32F w/d 1968/77
111-4 (JBU) PSUC1/3/Marshall B41D w/d 1975-7
115-6 (JBU) PSUC1/3/Pennine B41D w/d 1978

1965
121-30 (CBU-C) PDR1/ 1 Mk II/Roe H43/34F w/d 1978

1966
131-5 (GBU-D) PDR1/ 1 Mk II/East Lancs H43/34F w/d 1979
136-47 (GBU-D) PDR1/ 1 Mk II/Roe H43/34F w/d 1980

1967
148-52 (LBU-E) PDR1/ 1 Mk II/Neepsend H43/34F w/d 1980/1
153-60 (LBU-E) PDR1/ 1 Mk II/Roe H43/34F w/d 1980
117-20 (LBU-E) PSRC1/1/Marshall B45D w/d 1976 (33ft 6in long)

1967/68
161-71 (OBU-F) PDR1/1 Mk II/Roe H43/34F w/d 1980/81

1968
172-7 (OBU-F) PSUR1/1/Marshall B48+20D w/d 1974/5
(36ft long)

1969
178-82 (SBU-F) PDR1A/1/Roe H43/31D w/d 1981/2

1970
183-7 (WBU-H) PDR1A/1/Roe H43/31D w/d 1981/2

1971
188-99 (ABU-J) PDR1A/1/Roe H43/31D w/d 1982-4

Top: **Seen in the dingy backwater at Mumps where crew changeovers took place, Northern Counties-bodied PD2 no.460 here is in the 'pommard' livery.**
Ian Lynas

Above: 'Eeh lass, put t'babby in t'pram now we've gorroff this nice Roe-bodied PD3, number 105', she's probably saying – or probably not.

The PD3s had semi-automatic transmission, that is, featuring a four-speed direct-acting epicyclic gearbox with two-pedal control. Moreover, they reverted to 'exposed radiator' layout. Their Roe bodies were of high interior appointment, featuring up-to-date decor and other details. However, drivers disliked them for being 'poor pullers' with transmission slip. Conductors complained that the platform layout left them with nowhere to stand clear of passenger movement and of having to go upstairs to change the setting of the destination blind. Pedestrians complained about their squealing brakes!

The four batches of saloons (four Tiger Cubs then two more, four Panther Cubs and six Panthers) came equipped for operation by driver only. In 1964 Tiger Cub no.111 journeyed across Europe, visiting Oldham's twin town, Kranj, in the former Yugoslavia. Tiger Cubs nos.115/6 had bodywork built in Oldham by Pennine Coachcraft, an associate of Seddon Diesel Vehicles. At 7.7 tons the unladen weight of the Panther Cubs was relatively high for a chassis with the 6.54-litre engine.

OCPTD was rocked when in 1965 a Ministry of Transport vehicle examination resulted in immediate

Top: **The setting here may look like one of Oldham's more rural routes but Marshall-bodied Tiger Cub no.111 is seen when new in 1964 on its way across Europe to Yugoslavia.**
J J Holmes

Above: **The arrival of ten stylish new Roe-bodied Atlanteans – stylish for 1965 – clearly engendered much pride in the Oldham fleet. But the pride had a fall in the autumn of that year when 97 older buses were put off the road by the vehicle examiner.**
Oldham Evening Chronicle

Left: **It was no use his tugging, he couldn't pull it over and it would have been suicidal anyway. Besides, it was one of Sheffield Transport Department's buses loaned for the 1965 emergency, and they'd have been cross if Oldham had damaged it.**

Below: **In the pommard livery, new and modish Neepsend-bodied Atlantean 152 contrasts with its Glodwick Road environment.**
R H G Simpson

prohibition notices being imposed upon 97 buses – 42 per cent of the 233-strong fleet. Circumstantial evidence suggests that the action may have been a 'technical' one in response to a particular situation and indeed some of the faults had no serious safety implications, such as torn upholstery. The sense of shock, however, was profound. Service levels were maintained only by the hiring of 45 buses from other municipalities, although five of the suspended vehicles were rectified and returned to service on the same day and a further 42 within a week. Eight vehicles were withdrawn immediately. The borrowed buses comprised 32 Leylands from Bolton (6), Bury (2), Manchester (10), St Helens (3), Sheffield (5), Stockport (2) and Wigan (4); seven AECs from Bradford (3) and Rochdale (4); and six Daimlers from Salford.

One outcome of this event was the replacement of some older buses in 1965/66 by 16 acquired from other municipal operators, as detailed below. All had Leyland metal-framed bodies and were withdrawn 1968-70. No.463 (LWE 104) was a 1949 PD2/1 with H33/26R body, formerly Sheffield no.604; nos.464-6 (LWE 109-11), also ex-Sheffield (nos.609-11) were 1949 PD2/1s with H30/26R bodies. Nos.467-70 (ACP 392/85/8/90) were 1947/8 PD2/1s with H33/26R bodies, ex-Halifax nos.308/101/4/6. Nos.471-4 (DBN 329/30/7/42) were 1949 PD2/4s with H33/26R bodies,

ex-Bolton nos.426/7/34/8. Nos.475-8 (OWB 856/7/9/61) were 1952 PD2/10s with H33/26R bodies, ex-Sheffield nos.656/7/9/61. Nos.467-70 were prepared and repainted in Oldham livery by Halifax JOC, the others by Neepsend Coachworks.

In 1966 Oldham's livery was altered to Devon cream and pommard (a deep pink), and on double-deckers the cantrail-level band of the darker colour was omitted. Regarding the Roe bodywork on the Atlanteans, some details of the design were

Left: Many operators found Leyland Panthers troublesome and didn't keep them for very long, the PTE getting rid of the 1968 ex-Oldham half-dozen by 1975 although other operators persisted and made them work. Good-looking no.177 here progresses through Mumps. R H G Simpson

Below: Still serviceable despite being 18 years old when acquired in 1965 following the disastrous events, Leyland PD2/1 no.470 (previously Halifax no.106) is seen at Shaw (Wren's Nest terminus) with no.471, a 1949 PD2/4 (previously Bolton no.426).

incorporated in order to diminish somewhat the bland and boxy aspects of the design of many bodies on rear-engined chassis. The upper saloon windows were 4in deeper than those used in the standard Park Royal group design, but the main mitigating features were the v-shaped front windows of both saloons and the peak effect of the front dome (and rear one). Interior layout was well planned, featuring flat floors, extra luggage space and translucent roof panels.

The bodies of the second batch (nos.131-5) were built by East Lancashire Coachbuilders of Blackburn, that concern's first Oldham order, to a well-proportioned design developed from that specified previously by Bolton Corporation. A further five (nos.148-52) were of virtually identical appearance but built by East Lancashire's subsidiary, Neepsend Coachworks of Sheffield, for quicker delivery. Atlanteans numbered from 161 had the O.680-type 11.1-litre engine instead of the O.600-type 9.8.

From 1968 it became permissible for double-deckers to be crewed by driver only. Atlanteans from no.178 were therefore specified to have low destination screens at the front so as to be operable from the cab, to be suitable for the fitting of fare-taking and ticket-issuing equipment, and with centre exits to minimise the time spent at bus stops. Earlier Atlanteans also were adapted gradually, although remaining single-door and except for no.126, keeping their original destination fitment.

As from 1 November 1969 OCPTD ceased to exist and its operations came under the South East Lancashire and North East Cheshire Passenger Transport Executive, Southern Division. Atlanteans nos.183-7 were delivered to Selnec PTE as nos.5183-7 in OCPTD livery, and nos.188-99 were delivered to Selnec PTE as nos.5188-99 in Selnec livery. **CB**

Secondhand
THE TROLLEYBUS BOOM

There was a good market for trolleybuses with one careful owner, says MICHAEL DRYHURST

And why wouldn't you let this beauty pass? A driver can be seen lowering the the (secondhand) booms of Bournemouth no.288, in allowing right-of-way to no.285. While both buses are bodied by Weymann, no.288 is a 1947 BUT 9611T ex-Brighton, and no.285 is a 1959 Sunbeam MF2B, the latter possibly representing the apogee in excellence of British trolleybus design.
Photos by Michael Dryhurst except where indicated

THIRTY-FIVE YEARS HAVE PASSED SINCE THE last journey of a trolleybus on a UK public thoroughfare, and conventional wisdom is that those that were sold all ended up in Bradford. Well, a lot did. But a lot more didn't . . .

The first trolleybus to operate in the UK did so within the confines of the Hendon depot of the Metropolitan Electric Tramways when was undertaken some demonstration runs sometime during 1909, but within two years systems were inaugurated in both Bradford and Leeds (20 June 1911) followed by 19 others within the next 15 years. And while Bradford

was both the first and the last, many British pioneer systems did not last the course – Aberdare, Dundee, Halifax, Oldham, Rhondda, Stockport, etc. And most of that pioneer rolling-stock was scrapped. But . . .

Left: **With examples in the left foreground of Nuffield products and a Southdown Guy Arab III/Northern Counties, Brighton Corporation no.46, a 1947 BUT 9611T with Weymann bodywork, glides into Old Steine; it was sold in 1959 to Bournemouth Corporation.**

Below: **And Bournemouth took the three BH&D BUT 9611T, which with the four from BCT were the only two-axle double-deckers in this Hampshire fleet. With reconfigured destination screens, ex-BH&D no.6393/ Bournemouth no.294 heads towards the Square.**

replaced by motorbuses in June 1930. But York decided to upgrade the overhead and in 1931 took delivery of three Karrier E4/Roe single-deck trolleybuses; however an operating agreement concluded between York Corporation and the West Yorkshire Road Car Co. saw the end of trolleybuses and in 1935 the trio was sold to Chesterfield Corporation, lasting until closure of that system in 1938. While the two aforementioned systems closed in the 1930s, that decade saw the opening of some 18 trolleybus operations, with another 13 having survived from the previous decade. However, by the 1950s the trolleybus

After five years in storage after they were withdrawn from service, Halifax sold to Dundee its two 1912-built Railless cars, while the shortest-lived UK system (Rhondda, three months) sold its cars to contractor Clough Smith, which vehicles then were bought by the Teeside Railless Traction Board; and of the three Stockport vehicles, one was sold to the Mexborough & Swinton Tramways Co, which had become the first company-operated trolleybus entity in the UK. York Corporation had commenced trolleybus operation during December 1920, but this sole route was

was being re-assessed and the first casualty was Birmingham Corporation, which comparatively small system lasted 29 years, and while none of its final fleet saw further service as trolleybuses, in 1934 Birmingham had sold to Wolverhampton its 'odd-man-out' Sunbeam no.67. Thereafter, that decade saw another 10 UK systems discontinued, and of these, eight sold trolleybuses for further service.

Darlington had been an early convert, commencing operation on 17 January 1926, and until 1951 this corporation operated trolleybuses solely; conversion to

motorbus took place in stages, final closure coming on 31 July 1957. Sold to Bradford were 16 of the Karrier W single-deckers while nos.68-73, Darlington's only-double-deckers, moved down the A1 to Doncaster, where these BUT 9611T became nos.378-83,

Merged

Cleethorpes had commenced trolleybus operation in 1937, jointly with neighbouring Grimsby, which municipality had opened its system in 1926; the operators had merged their transport operations as of 1 January 1957, but the trolleybus system was abandoned on 4 June 1960. Sold to Bradford were five former Grimsby Karrier W/Roe H56R of 1946/47 while Walsall took six former Cleethorpes buses, four BUT 9611T/Northern Coachbuilders, and two Roe-bodied Crossley TDD42/3, the last 'genuine' trolleybuses of this make (later some 'BUT' trolleybus chassis were assembled at the Crossley works in Stockport). Earlier, in 1946, Cleethorpes had sold to Nottingham Corporation its nos.59-62, 1937 AEC 661T/Park Royal H56R.

Another early trolleybus convert was the Hastings Tramways Co, which commenced operations in April 1928 with an initial fleet comprising 58 Guy BTX three-axle vehicles – eight with Dodson O57R bodies, the remainder B37C-bodied by Ransomes, Sims & Jefferies. With invasion scares and wartime-imposed restricted access to the south coast, a number of vehicles was rendered surplus and sales took place,

all featuring the single-deck buses; in 1941 six went to Nottingham Corporation, a further six to Derby in 1942 while in 1943 a final half-dozen passed to the Mexborough & Swinton Traction Co. Replacement of the original fleet had started in 1939 and continued in 1946/48, and with closure of the system on 31 May 1959, all 25 postwar trolleybuses were sold, 12 to Bradford, eight to Walsall and five to Maidstone.

During the mainstream period of British trolleybus systems, there were five company-operated concerns, of which only one survived the 1950s. Llanelli & District Traction Co was a Balfour Beatty group subsidiary, operating trolleybuses for 20 years. With nationalisation of the electricity-generating industry in 1948, ownership of the company passed to the South Wales Electricity Board, which in turn sold it in 1952 to BET group affiliate South Wales Transport, which within nine months had discontinued trolleybus operations. At closure, two Karrier W/Roe UH56R were bought by Maidstone, while Bradford took the chassis of the other 10 Karrier W. Another Balfour Beatty trolleybus-operating entity was the Notts & Derby Traction Co, such operations commencing in January 1932. The keynote of this company was its 15-mile long interurban

Walsall no.309 was one of eight Hastings trolleybuses purchased from Maidstone & District. This 1963 view reveals extensive restructuring of the 1948-built Weymann body, while the (secondhand) booms have come to grief on the overhead.

route from Nottingham to Ripley; however, this ran through an area of much coal-mining which caused road subsidence and this was a major factor in the decision to abandon electric traction, which ended in April 1953. Back in 1937 N&D had sold to Mexborough six all-English Electric single-deckers, while the whole final fleet (18 AEC 661T, 15 BUT 9611T, all Weymann-bodied) was sold to Bradford.

Often overlooked is the fact that London Transport sold 130 trolleybuses for further service, all three-axle vehicles. In 1956, five C1-class (AEC 664T/MCCW H70R) dating from 1935 were sold to Georgetown, Malaya, while in 1961 was sold to nine various Spanish operators a total of 125 of the 127-strong Q1-class (BUT 9641T/MCCW H70R); of the remaining two, one was scrapped, the other preserved.

Pioneer systems

While Wales had seen (and lost) pioneer trolleybus systems at Aberdare and Rhondda and which by 1925 were but memories, perhaps it was predictable that when in September 1930 Pontypridd Urban District Council (the only UDC to operate trolleybuses) inaugurated its system it was proclaimed to be 'the first modern trolleybus system in Wales'. Who could argue with that? There were ambitious plans to link-up routes with Rhondda Tramways with which Pontypridd worked a joint tram route but on conversion the latter opted for motorbuses, and so Pontypridd was a one-trolleybus route of 3.3-miles length. Of the total of 17 trolleybuses

owned (of which no.9 was one of only two trolleybuses ever built by Bristol), no fewer than 15 were sold on to other operators. The initial fleet of seven English Electric B32C buses was sold in 1946 to Cardiff Corporation for its Docks route, where a low bridge precluded double-deckers, while of the eight Pontypridd austerity-specification double-decker trolleybuses left at closure (31 January 1957), four went to South Shields and two each to Doncaster, and Walsall.

Another pioneer system was St Helens, opening in 1927 and in operation for 31 years. While the first trolleybuses here were saloons, all subsequent deliveries were of double-deckers, to lowbridge configuration. However, in 1950/51, 16 highbridge trolleybuses were received, all bodied by East Lancashire Coachbuilders, the chassis order split evenly between BUT 9611T (H56R) and Sunbeam S4 (H55R). Upon closure, the Sunbeams went to South Shields, while the BUTs went to Bradford . . .

When reviewing UK trolleybus systems, it is somewhat surprising to realise how many were opened in the third decade of the 20th century, a total of 17; one such was that of Southend, in Essex, which opened in October 1925. During its 29 years of existence, this

Of the four ex-GCT former Cleethorpes BUT 9611T purchased by Walsall, three were subjected to extensive rebuilding whereby they were extended to 30ft length, and their H56R bodies became H69F, like no.875 seen here, or in the case of no.877, H67F.

Teesside Municipal Transport no.T291, a Sunbeam F4A with Burlingham H68F bodywork, supplied originally to Reading in 1961. This view was taken in November of 1987 when the now-preserved bus was used in the promotion of a book published by World of Transport, outside which Twickenham store the vehicle is seen, hence the route number set. The author of this piece is the modest chap on camera left.

T Wright

system operated some interesting vehicles, including the unique Gloucester TDD with Gloucester L54C body, an AEC Q 761T and the only vehicles to carry Strachans trolleybus bodies. Although discontinued in 1954, the first sale of Southend trolleybuses occurred in 1940 when nos.110/1, 1930-built English Electric H56D vehicles, were sold to Nottingham; during World War 2 Southend had received nine austerity trolleybuses, all of which were sold to Doncaster in 1953.

With regard to the 1960s, that decade might well be dubbed 'The Terminator', as during the period 21 systems succumbed, although there were still some trolleybus sales . . .

Interworked

The interworked systems of Ashton-under Lyne (small) and Manchester (large) closed on 31 December 1966; in 1960, Ashton had sold two Sunbeam/ Roe UH56R to Bradford. The Bournemouth system closed on 20 April 1969 and although the newest UK trolleybuses were operated here, some being only seven years old, they failed to find a buyer; however, in 1942 Bournemouth had sold to South Shields a 1933-built Thornycroft BD trolleybus with Brush B32C body. Brighton was served by two trolleybus operators, the Corporation and Tilling group company, Brighton Hove & District. While service had commenced in

1939, BH&D did not come on-line until March 1946. The system was closed in two stages, and immediately prior to Stage 1 in March 1959 all 11 BUT 9611T – 8 Corporation, 3 BH&D – were sold; of these, seven went to Bournemouth, two to Bradford, and two to Maidstone, and despite the fact that the eight BH&D AEC 661T trolleybuses had seen but 13 years' service, they went for scrap.

Huddersfield. The word always reminds me of a gross unrepeatable joke told by one Wolfgang Suschitzky, an extremely talented movie director of photography, whose son Peter follows in his footsteps. But I digress. To buttress the Reading trolleybus fleet, in the period 1948-51 Huddersfield sold to the Berkshire capital 12 three-axle Karrier E6 of 1934, which carried Brush H64R bodies, although only six of these vehicles actually saw service in Reading. Suffolk, Constable country – and one isn't talking PC49, hayricks or sailing barges, but a pioneer trolleybus system that relied solely on such vehicles during the 37 years from 1923 to 1950; at least its first motorbuses were of AEC manufacture . . . For most of its prewar rolling stock, Ipswich purchased from local company Ransome, Sims & Jefferies; however, wartime dictates saw Karrier as the Ipswich supplier, to be supplanted by Sunbeam. Twelve of the latter were supplied in

1950, of which at abandonment in 1963, eight passed to Walsall.

Mention has been made previously of the company trolleybus operators. Among these was the Mexborough & Swinton Traction Co. Sort of sandwiched between Rotherham (operating trolleybuses since 1912) and Doncaster (trolleybuses introduced 1928), M&S (trolleybuses since 1915) had grandiose plans for interworking with its neighbours, but in the event, only the Rotherham link was achieved (despite a test-run by a Doncaster double-deck trolleybus in mid-1928). By virtue of the fact that all of its trolleybuses were saloons, M&S remained unique, and this last bastion of BET trolleybuses closed in March 1961. In 1954 the company had sold to Doncaster nos.1-6 and on abandonment Bradford took 12; in both instances these 18 trolleybuses received new double-decker bodies.

Left: Nearly 300 trolleybuses were built during World War 2, all by Karrier/Sunbeam, of which a small proportion was single-deckers, either for Darlington or Mexborough & Swinton. Bodywork on these newly-constructed buses was by Brush, Roe or Park Royal, and typical of the Park Royal product is Doncaster no.392, a Sunbeam W, originally Southend no.138, which the Yorkshire operator subsequently had rebodied by Roe.

Below: Although it opened in 1936, the Reading Corporation trolleybus system had a greater proportion of postwar stock, although in 1948/49, 12 1934-built Karrier E6 with 64-seat Brush bodies were purchased from Huddersfield. Reading no.158 is seen at the General Station in September 1954. In the postwar period of trolleybus sales this was the only instance of three-axle double-deckers passing between UK operators.

Left: At abandonment in 1952, 12 Llanelli & District trolleybuses were sold, two as complete vehicles and 10 chassis to Bradford Corporation, which had them rebodied by East Lancs. Seen in August 1958 is Bradford Karrier W no.776, which had been Llanelli no.38, carrying a Roe utility body.

Below: The two complete Llanelli trolleybuses passed to Maidstone Corporation, where they retained their Roe austerity bodies. Maidstone no.84, ex-Llanelli no.40, is seen in February 1959.

Interestingly, the first Reading trolleybus route never saw public service; this was a former tram route that actually had been converted to motorbus operation, but upon which had been erected overhead to provide a training-ground for would-be trolleybus drivers. Excluding the initial fleet of 31 vehicles, in the period 1949 to 1961 Reading took delivery of 44 new trolleybuses, but on closure in November 1968, only five were sold on, these being part of the batch of 12 Sunbeam F4A supplied in 1961; the survivors passed to Teesside Municipal Transport.

Single-deckers

The fourth trolleybus system to open in Great Britain was that at Rotherham, on 3 October 1912, and this was also one of the longest-lasting, closure coming almost 53

years to the day after inauguration. Like neighbouring Mexborough & Swinton, Rotherham favoured single-deck trolleybuses, after World War 2 acquiring a fleet of 44 Daimler CTC/CTE6 buses fitted with East Lancs B38C bodywork; subsequently, it was figured that such vehicles were not optimising their full economic capability, as a result of which 20 were rebodied in 1956 with Roe H70R bodies. Not only did this result in some

impressive-looking vehicles, but also ensured almost another 10 years of existence of this interesting system. After this rebodying exercise, 24 single-deckers remained; eight were retained while the other 16 were exported to Spain, for operation in Cadiz.

Wolverhampton Corporation opened its trolleybus system in October 1923, and for a short time enjoyed the distinction of operating the largest such facility in the

Above: **When the St Helens trolleybus fleet closed in 1958 eight buses passed to Bradford and the rest, like no.201, formerly St Helens no.174, to South Shields. These eight Sunbeam F4 carried Northern Coachbuilders bodies.**

Right: **Don't be fooled by the open windscreen – this was an extremely nippy Saturday in December 1956. Delivered to Darlington Corporation in 1949 to become the first double-deck trolleybuses in that town, these six BUT 9611T/East Lancs were sold to Doncaster in 1952, where the former no.71 is seen at work, by now no.381; three years later, the batch was sold to Bradford ..**

world, by virtue of having reached its maximum route mileage in the mid-1930s. This system lasted 44 years, during the course of which some trolleybuses were sold on; in 1950 nine Sunbeam MF2/Park Royal H54R dating from 1938 passed to Southend, while in 1952 a further 11 (six Park Royal, five Roe) were purchased by Belfast, where they lasted but a very short time.

Bradford

Which brings us finally to … Bradford. Do I hear you say: 'But isn't this a piece about selling-on, not buying-in?' So it is. But in addition to purchasing nearly 90

… where five of the six were rebodied, also by East Lancs, though to a different body style and layout. With its new 66-seat forward entrance East Lancs body, Bradford no.832 was previously Doncaster no.380, and before that Darlington no.70.
John Fozard

used trolleybuses from 10 different owners, Bradford also sold some. In 1943 10 all-English Electric H56R buses dating from 1929/32 were sold to Newcastle upon Tyne were, while in 1945 another three such buses went to Tyneside, although in this instance to

South Shields. And it was to this municipality that Bradford made its first-ever trolleybus sale, when in 1942 the Yorkshire operator's AEC 761T Q went to South Shields (Note for Corgi/OOC. Any chance of the double-deck Q 0761 appearing in the trolleybus version? There were some 23, in a variety of liveries). And perhaps a case could be made that there has been further selling on? In preservation? Currently there is in preservation a total of 121 trolleybuses from UK operators, a stunning figure and a magnificent effort. Thank you, anybody and everybody (including those sadly no longer with us) involved in preserving these impressively-efficient and magnificent vehicles.

In conclusion, acknowledgment must be made of the invaluable help gleaned from the publications 'British Trolleybus Systems', Ian Allan Ltd, 1986; 'Crossley', Oxford Publishing Co, 2002; 'Preserved Buses', PSV

Upon abandonment of the Notts & Derby system, 30 of its trolleybuses were purchased by Bradford, 15 AEC and 15 BUT, all bodied by Weymann, and such was the similarity of the blue/cream livery worn by both operators that many of the N&D buses remained in that livery while with Bradford. Seen in February 1957 is ex-N&D AEC no.338, by now Bradford no.592 – still in N&D colours.

Circle, 2006; 'World Trolleybus Encyclopaedia', Trolleybooks 2000; and 'The London Trolleybus', Dryhurst Publications (who?), 1961.

And a confession. Despite being in my dotage, this is my first solo piece via a computer-operating system. Which I could not have achieved without the help, patience and long-suffering of the lady-wife Karen. Plus the occasional bottle of whisky. Occasional... **CB**

MILESTONES IN DOUBLE-DECK BUS DESIGN

GAVIN BOOTH nominates a trend-setting design

Bristol Lodekka

Was there life before the Lodekka?

Bristol, as a company in the Tilling Group, designed its models largely to meet the requirements of Tilling Group companies, though its products were widely used beyond the group. Rather like the Guy Arab, the Bristol K type, first introduced in 1937, was a bus that appealed to engineers, with its Gardner 5LW engine and constant mesh gearbox. The K5G was built until 1942 and Bristol reappeared with double-deck bus chassis in 1944 with the K6A, with AEC 7,7-litre engine. After World War 2 the K5G and K6A continued in production, to be joined in 1946 by the K6B, featuring Bristol's own AVW engine. From 1950 the longer KS and wider KSW models replaced the K, and production, with the same engine choices, continued until 1957.

By this time only state-owned companies could buy Bristol chassis as the Tilling Group had voluntarily sold out to the British Transport Commission in 1948, and what had been the most common chassis/body combination, Bristol/Eastern Coach Works, became the standard product. Many of the K type chassis had lowbridge ECW bodies with the side gangway layout popularised by Leyland's Titan TD1, as many of the Tilling Group fleets operated in more rural areas where low railway bridges were much in evidence. The lowbridge layout with its four-across seating was awkward for passengers and conductors and Bristol and ECW worked hard to develop a new low-built model that would allow normal seating on both decks in a body no higher than 13ft 6in (4.1m). The result,

The Lodekka looked suitably rugged; this is an early Hants & Dorset LD6B with its single-deck contemporary from the Bristol/ECW stable, a Wilts & Dorset LS, behind.

perhaps surprising from a traditional and conservative builder, was the Lodekka, the first lowheight double-decker to go into full production.

So, what was different about the Lodekka?

A great deal. The first two prototype Lodekkas, built in 1949/50, achieved the low overall height with complex transmission arrangements, but the production models, from 1953, had dropped-centre double-reduction rear axles that allowed the lower deck floor to be flat from platform level, and this allowed a normal-depth upper deck with a centre gangway and two-and-two seating. The production ECW body, 13ft 4in (4.06m) high, had deep windows on both decks and was typically delivered with 58 or 60 seats, and open or enclosed rear platforms.

Mechanically the Lodekka was clearly the successor to the K type, with Bristol AVW (or later, BVW) or Gardner 5LW or 6LW engines, and a constant mesh gearbox.

As longer buses were permitted, longer Lodekkas were produced, but a major change came in 1959 with the F series, which featured a truly flat lower deck floor and air suspension of the rear axle. The longer FLF model with forward entrance became the most popular model, and in its later years Gardner 6LX and Leyland 600 engines were available, as were semi-automatic gearboxes.

The Lodekka sold to Tilling and Scottish group companies in substantial numbers, and the model was discontinued in 1968.

Where Bristol went, did others follow?

Yes, but never with the same success. AEC and Park Royal developed a lowheight model, the Bridgemaster, built between 1958 and 1963 in various lengths and body layouts. Dennis decided, not unreasonably, that the Lodekka might appeal to companies that were not in state ownership, and so entered an agreement to build the Lodekka under licence as the Loline. It enjoyed some success with BET Group, municipal and even independent customers. Leyland developed a model largely aimed at the Scottish Bus Group, which had been a good customer for lowbridge Titans, but which was also buying Lodekkas. The Lowlander, introduced in 1961, was actually designed and built at

Top: The Lodekka got round the awkward lowbridge side-gangway arrangement that had been necessary to keep overall height down. This is a Yorkshire Traction all-Leyland PD2.

Above: The air-suspended flat-floor F series Lodekkas took the concept a stage further. This is a 1965 York West Yorkshire FS6B in York in 1979.
Gavin Booth

Albion's works near Glasgow, and was badged as an Albion in Scotland and a Leyland elsewhere. AEC's integral Bridgemaster was replaced in 1962 by the Renown chassis. Guy's Arab MkV of 1962 had a lower frame, though not as low as the Lodekka and the like.

None of these models survived beyond the end of the 1960s, though, as the government's scheme for New Bus Grants encouraged operators to buy buses suitable for driver-only operation, which at the time meant rear-engined models, and the Daimler Fleetline and, to a lesser extent, the Leyland Atlantean had picked up the lowheight mantle. **CB**

GONE BUT NOT FORGOTTEN

DAVID THROWER looks back fondly at London's T and TD classes

T719 stands in the sunshine on route 213, at the well-remembered stop at North Cheam ('Queen Vic'), on Norbiton garage's duty 1 on 28 June 1952. Sid's Snack Bar in the background (was it run by Sidney James when he worked with Tony Hancock, as a sideline?) doubtless did good business from bus crews.
Photos by Alan B Cross, except where indicated

DURING THE EARLY AND MIDDLE DECADES of the 20th century London Transport was always characterised by the classic double-decker, first the LT, ST and STL types and later the RT and then Routemaster families of designs. However, the single-deck fleet, particularly in the decades immediately preceding and following World War 2, was not without interest.

The prewar single-deck London Transport fleet was dominated by a range of fascinating and sometimes very novel types of bus. There were the ageing 'Scooter' three-axle LT types, these being the single-deck equivalent of the Renown double-deckers, together with a great family of T type Regals, plus the much more unconventional TF (underfloor flat-engined), CR (rear-engined) and Q (side-engined) classes. The postwar single-deck fleet was of course dominated by the two great standardised classes, of the AEC RF in its various forms and the famous GS Guy.

But there was an interesting filling within this sandwich, which related to the decade of the 1940s, between the final handsome but conventional 10T10 Regals having arrived in 1938/39 and the first strikingly modern-looking RFs arriving in 1951. This was a quartet of non-standard and basically off-the-peg traditional designs, comprising two very distinctive

variants of AEC T type Regals, and two much more subtly-differentiated types of Leyland TD Tiger.

In summary, the four types of bus comprised as follows: AEC T type, fleetnumbers T719-68, with Weymann's so-called 'frowning' body design (total 50); AEC T type, fleetnumbers T769-98, with Mann Egerton (non-frowning) bodies (total 30); Leyland TD type, fleetnumbers TD1-31, with Weymann (frowning) bodies (total 31); and Leyland TD type, fleetnumbers TD32-131, with Mann Egerton (non-frowning) bodies (total 100) – a grand total of 211 buses.

The four sub-classes were thus made up of the permutations achieved by intermixing two chassis makes (of three different detailed designs, as is explained later) and two body makes.

Confusingly, the denomination 'T' did not differentiate the two AEC sub-classes from each other or, worse still, from the plethora of prewar T sub-classes. Some of the latter had been part of the programme of standardisation embarked upon during the 1930s following London Transport's formation, whilst others had come from independent operators.

The two new Leyland TD classes were much more similar to each other than the two new AEC T classes were, so lumping those together under one class mattered less. As it happened, there were no prewar TD single-deckers, but confusingly for enthusiasts the letters had previously been used on the various sub-classes of Leyland TD1 double-deck Titans of the late 1920s and early 1930s that had been inherited from independents in 1933. These had only been withdrawn and sold by the start of the 1940s, so it was perhaps surprising to see the letters being re-used so very soon afterwards.

The 14T12 Regals

First to be delivered to LT, at a time when serviceable buses were desperately needed, were the 14T12 Regals. These Regal I buses were just under 27ft 6in long, with

T732 on Sidcup's duty 2, is seen at Chislehurst on the busy route 228, also on 28 June 1952. The design of destination blinds on these vehicles resulted in a very crowded script, with (in this instance) no fewer than 14 words, plus route number, on a single panel, making them near-unreadable.

a wheelbase of 17ft 6in. Their width was actually just a shade under the maximum permitted of 7ft 6in, and they weighed in unladen at a quite modest six tons, well within the capabilities of their relatively-small (by RT/RF standards) AEC A173-type 7.7 diesel engines.

Gear change was 'clash' (to use LT parlance) in all gears, marking a brief and doubtless unwelcome return to early-1930s practice after the years of introducing preselectors and epicyclic or torque converter gearboxes. The characteristic deep provincial-style AEC radiator rather than the low-mounted RT design was fitted, adding to the already-dated appearance of these buses, whilst the front wings, so unlike those of the handsome prewar 10T10 Regals, were a further giveaway that these buses were not London thoroughbreds. The 14T12, well-built and rugged as it might have been, was in truth little more than a slightly updated off-the-peg prewar model.

A sign perhaps of continuing post-wartime austerity was the lack of the familiar oval bonnet numberplate, the transfers being applied directly to the removable engine compartment side-panel. This latter practice could well have led to the occasional identity mix-up between different buses of the class during maintenance.

The Weymann bodywork seated 35 passengers, but this was to be reduced to 33 from 1949 onwards. Its most familiar feature was the aforementioned 'frowning' aspect of the front dome, which dipped downwards across the vehicle front. Personally, I have always really thoroughly liked this feature, which gave the buses a rather stylish and distinctive appeal. The blinds displayed were of the old prewar style layout,

with no fewer than four lines of information, making them decidedly crowded to read from a distance.

At the rear, a one-piece D-shaped window was a relapse from the distinctive three-piece design of the Q and LTC types, with their central emergency exit, to a more provincial styling. On the 14T12, the emergency exit was actually on the offside, immediately behind the rear axle, as on so many other non-London bus designs before and since. A notable feature was the use of horizontal sliding windows, instead of the more usual pinch-type or wind-down type half-drop saloon windows.

As befitted their intended Central Area fleet's use, the front entrances were open, without doors, nor was there any bodyside recess for a door. Passengers were shielded (probably far too strong a word) from the incoming gale by a half-bulkhead, but in winter these would have been very cold buses indeed to work or travel on, and of course they also had no saloon heaters.

Other small features that helped to 'Londonise' the design included the use of a very small circular nearside mirror (a little larger than that used by a dentist, but I am only exaggerating slightly), the fitting of a spring-loaded holder at roof level, just above the entrance, to carry route number stencils, and of course the familiar garage running-number stencil holders at waist level. These fittings were also later to be applied from new to the two variants of TD Tigers and to the 15T13 Regals.

Finally, the 14T12s established two features that were to become indelibly linked with the golden age of London Transport. Externally, they established the new postwar Central Area bus livery of red with simple cream lining-out, a livery that was to continue undisturbed until the replacement of cream (by this time on just the RT, RLH, RF and incoming Routemaster families) by flake grey lining, during the 1960s.

Internally, they inaugurated what must surely be the world's most famous public transport seat moquette of all time, which was to become so indelibly associated with the RT, RF, and GS families, and which mercifully never altered until the final end of the RT and RF in traffic in 1979. One can calculate that eventually anything up to half a million examples of seat squabs or backs must have been in existence at any one time in the 1950s with this pattern of moquette, and yet it was very quietly launched in 1946 by this perhaps most unlikely of candidates.

Into traffic

The closing years of the 1940s and the start of the 1950s were a period of constant upheaval in the LT fleet, as the incoming T, TD and then RF types progressively displaced the prewar LT, T, Q, TF and CR classes. These changes were rarely straightforward, usually involving many successive re-allocations and route conversions as engineers struggled to give the crews the best vehicles available, or sometimes, simply enough vehicles at all, at a time of huge travel demand.

The first 14T12 to arrive was T726, which entered Chiswick for licensing (this was still in the pre-Aldenham era) in March 1946, followed by 17 more by the end of April. The first 14T12 buses actually into traffic were those delivered to Uxbridge garage for route 223, to Kingston for routes 201, 215 and 219, and to Muswell Hill for route 212. The fact that these deliveries took place less than a year after the cessation of hostilities in Europe speaks very well of the bus manufacturing industry's' determination to restore normality quickly.

These initial deliveries were rapidly followed by the arrival of more at Kingston and Uxbridge, with additional deliveries in June 1946 at Kingston and at Muswell Hill. In July, yet more went to Kingston.

September deliveries went to Muswell Hill again. My late grandfather, a foreman at Weymann's coachworks, used to fondly recall these happy times, with new buses being turned out at unprecedented rates and with huge queues of orders from clamouring customers. As 1946 drew to a close, the last half-dozen 14T12s were delivered to Muswell Hill and to Uxbridge.

The arrival of these first new vehicles, off-the-peg or not, was a vital step forward for London Transport, struggling as it was with an ageing fleet still visibly suffering from the backlog of wartime maintenance. The 14T12s were London's first new single-deckers for almost six years, and if LT had been able to obtain more, it would probably have gladly done so.

By the end of 1946 the Muswell Hill contingent had been moved to Uxbridge and Kingston, with some vehicles going to Sidcup for route 228. By May 1952, a new garage at Norbiton was to replace Kingston, using 14T12 buses for routes 201, 206 and the longer east-west route 213. The type, together with some prewar 10T10 ex-Green Line Regals demoted to bus work, also took over workings on route 264 after the weak Walton Bridge had been replaced by a new temporary structure. Sidcup's 14T12s then moved to Southall for route 211, whilst the type was displaced from the busy 213 by incoming RF Regals. A solitary 14T12 also went to South Croydon garage for route 234.

The reign of the 14T12 was to go into decline almost as soon as it had peaked, however, as various routes were converted to double-deck operation, releasing TD Leylands which in turn displaced 14T12 Regals.

The first retreat of the 14T12s came in late 1954, with TDs taking over routes 201, 206 and 264 at Norbiton, and with the redundant Regals being put up for disposal.

At Uxbridge, the Regals lost out early in 1955 when route 224A was introduced, operated by double-deckers, enabling 14T12 route 224 to be reduced in frequency. Other Uxbridge 14T12 routes, the 222, 224, 224A and 224B, were to continue, but these duties ended in November 1958 as a result of the making surplus of some RFs and a number of other types of bus after the calamitous seven-week bus strike earlier in the summer. Even at the tender age of 12 years, the 14T12 type was already dead.

The Weymann TD Tigers

The initial batch of 31 Leyland front-engined Tigers, coded 1TD1, were again a fraction under 26ft long, and again offered a 17ft 6in wheelbase. The buses had a four-speed constant-mesh (crash or 'clash') gearbox and servo vacuum brakes. Power was the then-standard Leyland E181 7.4-litre engine, offering just marginally less power than its AEC rival. Overall weight was one hundredweight more than the AEC, at 6 tons 2 cwt.

The Weymann 'frowning' bodywork fitted to this initial batch of TDs was identical in almost every respect to that fitted to the 14T12 Regals, and again featured the distinctive frontal appearance of roof dome and destination box, and the breezy entrance without doors.

The frowning Weymann front was one of two features to distinguish the buses immediately from the later Mann Egerton TD batch, the other being the chromed Leyland radiator shell, a feature that was not normally associated with London buses but which was also present on the Tiger's double-deck London Transport equivalent, the postwar STD batch. Livery was plain red with a very thin cream bead immediately below and above the windows. A minor point of note

The sleek lines of the postwar RT made the 14T12 design seem very elderly by comparison. Here, T758 waits at Uxbridge Station on route 224B on 10 July 1957, surrounded by members of the 7,000-strong RT family.

was that early deliveries had unpainted chromed driver's windscreens.

Seating capacity was a modest 33, later reduced in 1954 to 32 by singling the seat opposite the entrance, presumably to improve circulation space for the conductor and for standing passengers.

The buses were numbered TD1-31 and were very unmemorably registered HGF 959-89. Bodies were numbered 1305-35 in the LT body numbering scheme. It is not thought that any of the AECs and Leylands actually exchanged bodies during their lives, and in any case the careers of both batches were largely over before the famous Aldenham Works overhaul-cycle process was under way.

The very first bus to arrive, logically enough, was TD1, received at Chiswick at the start of December 1946, with nine more arriving by the end of the year. The whole batch when delivered went to Muswell Hill garage for route 212, arriving in full by mid-1947. These displaced the less-powerful 14T12s, as already noted, and also partially replaced three-axle LT single-deckers on route 210. Single-deckers were necessary on the busy 212 due to a weak bridge in Muswell Hill. The TDs were also used on routes 244, which had a restricted-height bridge in Green Dragon Lane, Grange Park, and on the 251.

The Weymann TD era at Muswell Hill was not to last for long without disturbance from the incoming horde of underfloor RF type buses for the Central Area. Route 210 went RF in late 1952, followed by route 212, enabling the displaced TDs to migrate either south-westwards to what was to ultimately become one of their two great spiritual homes, Kingston (the other eventually being Edgware), or eastwards to Loughton, where they saw use on routes such as the 254.

A Changing World

The brave new postwar world so long awaited by London Transport went beyond its passenger-demand peak almost before it was realised. Unprecedented

late-1940s demand for Central Area bus travel was all too soon being simultaneously weakened by rising car ownership, the arrival of the new-fangled television (particularly beyond the mid-1950s, when commercial television commenced), and other demographic and settlement changes, including the establishment of the ring of New Towns around London.

This latter factor, including the establishment of new employment, was to affect the older inner urban areas more than the outer-suburban TD territory, but it added to the general decline in Central Area ridership, releasing still-new double-deckers to assist in the policy of converting increasingly-busy outer suburban routes to RT and RTL operation. Central Area single-deck operations were to thus fall back from their originally-projected levels, and inevitably this meant an early decline for the TD fleet.

The TD, and the T, fleets were also earmarked for early withdrawal by the busmen's union, the Transport & General Workers' Union, which had a very significant influence over London Transport in the allocation of particular types of bus, particularly those which fell below the 'gold standard' of the RF and RT. The crash gearboxes and limited capacity of the TD meant that in terms of driving it was certainly far below the standards of the luxurious RF.

And, although it was against the rules for crews to converse whilst the bus was on the road ('A conductor … shall not when the vehicle is in motion distract the Driver's attention without reasonable cause or speak to him unless it is necessary to do so in order to give directions as to the stopping of the vehicle' – PSV Regulations, repeatedly reinforced in traffic circulars), doubtless crews appreciated being able to pass the time in conversation at quieter moments on the new RFs. This was something that the TD of course precluded, though this aspect of their case could hardly have been aired officially in any arguments by the union.

This would gradually result in TD operations prematurely becoming even more of a niche market by

Also at Uxbridge Station, T764 waits on route 223, Uxbridge garage's duty 8. RT1903 stands behind on route 204.

the late 1950s, often dependent upon some external factor such as continued restrictions upon a bridge on the route. In any case, the TD was now quite a small bus by single-deck standards.

Withdrawal of the 1TD1 type therefore commenced in 1956, the point at which the first general withdrawals in the overall postwar fleet began. The very first to go was TD12 in summer 1956, and the seven lowest-numbered were also all withdrawn by August 1956. Nevertheless, the type continued to be introduced in its twilight years to routes hitherto operated by other types, for example at Uxbridge, where they were used to supplement the 14T12s. However, the end was not far away, and the very last 1TD1 was withdrawn in early 1958 from Kingston garage.

The Later TD Tigers

The Mann Egerton-bodied TD type has always been a personal favourite. For many years, the late-lamented Kingston bus station has had an immortal image of a row of smart red RF types poking out into Clarence Street. But for those of us who are slightly longer in the tooth, Kingston epitomised the TD. Shopping meant Bentalls, Bentalls meant Kingston, and Kingston meant four or five of those funny old halfcab single-deckers, quite unlike anything else ever seen by childhood eyes in other parts of South London, lurking amongst the shafts of sunlight, in what was meant to be a public bus station but which was all but indistinguishable from the running garage further within. For a generation of enthusiasts, this made Kingston somewhere really special, with hanging around the bus station a gleeful alternative to being dragged round shopping.

The large 100-strong batch of these later TD single-deckers, coded 1/1TD2 by London Transport in its usual esoteric manner, presented an immediately-differing aspect to the trained enthusiast eye, with their neat Mann Egerton bodywork and featuring the solid cast-aluminium design of radiator surrounds, which was less prone to minor damage. The bodywork presented a less archaic appearance by 1948 standards than did the earlier 14T12 and 1TD1 dinosaurs, with a straightened-out roof line, no 'frown', and for the first time on the type, a proper oval bonnet-mounted fleetnumber plate.

Always an intriguing feature of the Mann Egerton TD batch was the provision of a nearside bodywork recess, to accommodate the doors that were still banned on Central Area buses by the Metropolitan Police. This meant that these bodies exactly matched the external profile of those fitted to the 15T13 Country Area buses described later, only lacking the actual door.

A further intriguing feature was that seating capacity was only 31 from the outset, rather than the Weymann batch's 33/32, by replacing transverse seats with longitudinal seats over the rear wheel arches. Again during 1954, this capacity was further reduced by one to 30, thus making the 1/1TD2 a very small bus indeed for crew operations, compared with the (initial) 41 capacity of an RF, and offering only a meagre four more seats than the one-man operated GS. Indeed, with a crew of two, the passenger seats per crew

member ratio of the TD after this modification was even lower than those woefully-inadequate and best-forgotten 16-seat Transit-conversion minibuses of the early deregulation era. And driver-only operation was never going to be possible with a TD . . .

Into Service

The 1/1TD2 batch arrived between October 1948 and October 1949, the initial lucky recipients being Hornchurch (route 250 and later routes 247 and 248) and Ponders End, Enfield, for routes 205 and 242, later also including the short-shuttle 243 between

Waltham Abbey and Waltham Cross. As elsewhere, the problem with the Enfield network of routes was a weak bridge, though subsequent road improvements enabled the Enfield Tigers to later be displaced in May 1953. Some of these Enfield routes were picturesque and rural, perhaps the nearest the TD ever really came to country bus operations.

In late 1948, TD deliveries went to Romford for two fairly local routes, the 247 to Brentwood and the 248 to Cranham, though the 247 was soon to be double-decked, whilst the 248 was converted to lowbridge RLH operation in 1955. Those TD buses displaced in

early 1950 were then to take over route 238, Noak Hill to Gidea Park. It is now largely forgotten that the outer parts of the North-East quadrant of LT operations became quite prolific TD territory during the early 1950s.

Early in 1949, further deliveries enabled the new TD buses to operate from Hanwell on route 211, between Ealing Broadway and Ruislip Station and Lido, and

Top: TD26 and TD21 stand alongside each other on 2 May 1953, with an RT behind on route 134. Note the different designs of blind, with four lines of wording on TD26 and only three, less crowded, lines on TD21.

Above: The Mann Egerton TDs ushered in a neater and less fussy frontal appearance, although they still looked dated compared with the prewar Q and postwar RF styling. Here, TD37, an early delivery, works route 243 on 2 May 1953.

Harrow Weald on the 221 and 230. The Ruislip section was soon afterwards cut back to Greenford.

The final new deliveries of the 1/1TD1 type were then delivered to Leyton and Tottenham garages to enable 'Scooter' AEC Renowns to be removed from route 236 from Leyton to Stroud Green.

The type of route operated by the TD class was now firmly established, usually being relatively moderately-trafficked outer suburban or semi-rural duties, with the very busy Muswell Hill and Leyton-Stroud Green operations being untypical.

The arrival of the Mann Egerton TD type at Kingston, which in later years was to influence one small boy's shopping habits so significantly, came in 1949 when Kingston received a batch to enable the conversion of the 201 and 216, though they also worked the 206, 213, 215 and 219. The 213 never actually received an allocation of the type, changing directly from use of the LT 'Scooter' six-wheelers and the 14T12s to new RFs. However, TD appearances were not uncommon, thus taking the design as far south as Belmont.

Further buses also went to Muswell Hill, these being the first of the Mann Egerton-bodied examples to join the large existing fleet of Weymann TDs there.

In mid-1949, another allocation that was to have long-term significance for LT enthusiasts took place, this being the delivery of a batch to Edgware for routes 240 and 240A, though the 240 was soon cut back and double-decked, the 240A being extended and increased in frequency to compensate. Once again, the problem was a bridge, this time a restricted-height underbridge at Mill Hill Broadway station.

Other buses went to Tottenham and to Leyton for route 236, a route that was to be famous many years later as the last crew-operated doorless RF route.

As early as 1950, the first full year of the entire batch being in service, allocation upheavals were to see the TD type ousted by double-deckers on route 247 at Hornchurch, whilst TDs also went to Hornchurch's route 238. Other TDs were drafted into Muswell Hill to replace the last of the three-axle Renowns there. Such reshuffling was to continue throughout the early 1950s as prewar single-deckers were sent for scrap or resale and LT's single-deck operations assumed their comfortably-familiar 1950s ambience.

The very last TD of the Mann Egerton batch, TD131, entered service at Tottenham in October 1949. The fleet was certainly being put to good use. The scheduled requirement for weekday operations at the close of 1949 was for the full 131 Tigers of the two variants, with none spare, reflecting the heavy passenger demand and the shortage of modern rolling stock. It was to remain at this level for several years to come.

Increasingly, the Mann Egerton and Weymann batches of the TD type became intermixed. A new recipient of the TD class, new in every sense, was the garage constructed at Norbiton, barely a stone's throw from the cramped premises at Kingston. When it opened in May 1952, Norbiton's workings were to include route 201. The type was also now to fully take over at Kingston on routes 215, 218 and 219, replacing prewar 4Q4 buses, whilst Kingston was to later add a new route 215A to its TD operations.

Space does not permit recounting every individual
stage of the movements of the TD fleet (both
Weymann- and Mann Egerton-bodied) through the
first part of the 1950s, and readers wishing to research
this should consult the excellent documentation
produced by Capital Transport and the London
Omnibus Traction Society during the past couple of
decades.

It is also recorded that occasionally the type was to
stray onto unusual workings – in retrospect, extremely
unusual, in view of LT's straitjacketed allocating of
particular types of bus to particular duties – with, for
example, a Kingston TD operating on double-deck
route 131, and at least two recorded instances of the
type finding itself on the Green Line network when a
failure in service had occurred. However, some
apparently rare workings were in fact part of normal
scheduling, for example the use in the early 1950s of a
Romford North Street TD on the otherwise RTL 247A.

Decline

Even as late as the end of 1953, when the full strength
of the RF fleet was in place, the TDs, both Weymann
and Mann Egerton varieties, were by no means
marginalised or seriously under-deployed, with over
100 needed in peak Monday to Friday traffic. But
decline was just around the corner, and slack, in the
form of stored vehicles, began to mount up, even this
early in the TDs' potential service life.

The Mann Egerton 1/TD2s were nevertheless to
continue to provide a useful part of the LT single-deck
Central Area fleet, even in the mid 1950s, when they
were initially used simply to displace the Weymann
variety. A further new area of TD operations was
inaugurated in early 1958 when the type replaced the
14T12 Regals at Uxbridge, as noted earlier, on route
224, 224A and 224B.

An interesting might-have-been was contemplated in
1954, this being the transfer of 25 of the anticipated
growing surplus of TDs to the Private Hire fleet,
thereby releasing all of the short 27ft 6in RF batch,
RF1-25, for Green Line duties. This startling proposal
was not implemented, for the very obvious reason that
a TD, even in 1954, was hardly private hire material.

Barely a decade after their introduction, the TD had
therefore become very much an oddity in the LT
Central Area bus scene, and of course much of LT's
territory, including the entire Country Area, had never
witnessed the TD at all. By mid-1954, at the height of
its operations with LT, the TD could still only be found
at just nine Central Area garages, these being
(clockwise) Muswell Hill, Tottenham, Leyton,
Loughton, Romford, North Street, Kingston, Harrow

Weald and Edgware. Harrow Weald was to lose its operation of the type on route 221 in November 1954.

Even by this time, these limited operations therefore made them rather special. One vast area that all but missed any TD presence at all was the whole south-east quadrant of the Central Area, where just two TDs had operated for a bare five weeks on route 256 between Shooters Hill and Woolwich before being displaced by double-deckers.

However, the shrinking of even the Mann Egerton TD operations was to continue, and by the final months of 1958 they were reduced to just five garages, these being in clockwise order Romford North Street, Norbiton, Kingston, Uxbridge and Edgware. The weekday schedules at that time required a total of just over 70 buses.

The TD empire was soon to shrink even further, with operations ending in mid-1959 at North Street, at Norbiton on routes 206 and 264, at Kingston on route 216 (the 216 following the two Norbiton routes after a month's delay awaiting vehicles) and at Uxbridge on the 224 group of routes.

These conversions alone reduced the number of licensed TDs by 21 buses. After a further lull, in early 1960 Kingston was also able to convert routes 218 and 219. However, as one of those curiosities that made Kingston such an interesting place for the enthusiast over the decades, the TD type was still retained for routes 215 and 215A, and TD operations also continued at Edgware on route 240A, reducing the total scheduled TD requirement to just nineteen.

The 215/A operation is reported to have been kept on at Kingston because of the small and supposedly more manoeuvrable size of the TD compared with the RF, though in retrospect this seems quite odd. After all, the two buses were of the same width, and although the RF was 4ft longer than the TD, the RF's

TD103 waits alongside TD121 for its next run on route 240A, in the final years of TD operations on this service.
David Thrower collection

set-back front axle actually made its wheelbase over 1ft shorter. The supposed difficulties of RF operation were therefore probably overstated, and in fact Kingston began to operate the 215 with RF buses on Sundays, with their quieter road conditions.

The final end at Kingston came (apparently without ceremony) at the close of February 1962, with the withdrawal of the remaining five TDs, by this time looking their age by London standards. One can well imagine that such an event nowadays would be marked by the partial repainting of the last five vehicles for a ceremonial run, followed by official preservation by LT of the best one and private preservation of the other four, but the last day at Kingston seems to have somehow passed completely unmarked.

The very last TD of all in service with London Transport is reported to have been TD124 on the 240A at Edgware on 9 October 1962. With this also almost-unnoticed event, the TD era, and indeed the whole period of operation of the immediate-postwar off-the-peg London bus, was at an end. At the close of 1962, just 13 delicensed examples still remained in LT ownership awaiting disposal.

But they weren't entirely forgotten by the platform staff, and in the late 1960s, a 'clippie' on my local Kingston RT route 71 regaled me with anecdotes from the TD era, the class already even by that time seeming to epitomise a long-lost age.

The 15T13 Regals

The 15T13 batch of AEC Regals was the fourth of this quartet of designs to arrive upon the London

A fine study of TD97 at Loughton Station when working route 254 on 2 May 1953.

Transport scene, and as already noted, effectively combined the TD-type Mann Egerton body with an AEC postwar Regal III chassis.

The buses set a higher standard of comfort than the earlier AEC Weymann-bodied 14T12 products, and also featured preselect gears, a key design requirement for a London bus, but one that later would not save them from relatively premature withdrawal. They still made a very fine note on which to end the long ancestry of the T class Regal in the London Transport fleet.

And somehow, unlike the 14T12s, these rather provincial-appearance buses managed to look part of the LT pedigree fleet from the outset. The AEC chassis was powered by the A208 engine, giving 9.6 litres, 25 per cent more than the 14T12s, though the overall weight was also higher than the earlier design, at 6 tons 11 cwt unladen. Braking was by air pressure, which of course also operated the gearbox.

An interesting aspect of the buses in this batch was that they used a chassis that extended right to the rear of the vehicle, it not being thought worthwhile to provide a shortened-tail chassis for a batch of only 30 buses. London Transport by this time normally favoured what would now be termed a 'crumple zone', without chassis at the rear, to absorb collisions in an era when stone setts and non-Macadamised roads made rear-end impacts due to skidding more common.

The front entrance was this time able to incorporate a manually-operated sliding door, as the entire class was intended from the outset for the Country Area. Livery was in the then standard Lincoln green, but with the old-style white relief around the windows, making these buses a particularly attractive product when new. These were the last deliveries to carry this livery.

As with the other batches, initial licensing checks were undertaken at Chiswick, before the buses, with their RT-like registrations HLX 439-68, entered service. Initial deliveries were to Hemel Hempstead in early 1948 for routes 307, 307A, 317, 322, and 377, with later deliveries going to Watford Leavesden Road for route 309.

The entire batch of the 15T13 Regals was in service by the end of 1948. The arrival of the new Regals released Q types for use elsewhere, in turn releasing hired-in buses back to their operators after London Transport's dire postwar vehicle shortage. Another type to be replaced was the unpopular 11T11 prewar Regal.

Later, the Watford batch moved over to the new Garston garage, for route 318. Several buses also went south to Crawley for routes 426, 434 and 473, the 434 taking them as far east as Edenbridge and the 473 as far south as Horsham. Later still, the Garston buses moved to Amersham for route 394.

In theory, the 15T13s should have given good service right up to the point where one-man operations became universal for single-deckers in the Country Area. They were well-powered and solidly built. But the flood of RF deliveries, backed by the 84-strong GS fleet, meant that the 15T13s were doomed to become a small class of non-standard buses.

Gradually, the impact of this very small batch of useful little buses was to be lost, as they slowly became scattered in penny numbers around the system, often operating on quiet 'backwater' routes such as the 377A, a Hemel Hempstead works service that did not even appear on bus maps, the even more obscure 391 to Batford Mill, and Garston's 318A and 318B. Many enthusiasts probably never saw any, unless they

All too often, photographers forget to bother with rear views, which causes preservationists great difficulty when restoring buses, years later. Fortunately, Alan Cross was more thorough, and here we see the rear end of TD65 at Ealing Broadway when working on route 211 on the 16 February 1952.

specifically tracked examples down when illicitly visiting garages. Just very occasionally, one would stray from its usual haunts if deployed on Green Line relief work, and the buses were even sometimes rarely used on special duties, such as private hire outings.

However, in the pecking-order of Country Area single-deckers, the 15T13 was under threat both from above and below. For instance, Hemel Hempstead's route 317 was to be converted in 1956 to driver-operated RFs, as was Amersham's route 394A.. Alternatively, an example of the little GS replacing its larger compatriot was route 361, Chorleywood Station to Rickmansworth, where the crew-operated 15T13 type was removed as an economy measure in 1954.

In 1956, two buses went to Kingston, still in green livery, and later were joined by a third bus, to augment the TD fleet there on its own soon-to-diminish network of routes. The three were then transferred to Norbiton for route 201, continuing oddities in a sea of red.

At the end of 1956, the weekday schedules still demanded a respectable 14 of these buses, but 12 months later this had sunk to a bare seven. Some of the Regals, still only a decade old, became staff buses at Reigate, Hackney and elsewhere. Inevitably, sales commenced, and numbers steadily shrank.

The three green 15T13s on loan to Norbiton were replaced by RF type buses in early 1959, signalling the end of T type operations in the Central Area. Full-scale 15T13 operation on route 426 at Crawley ended in late 1957, though one or two buses lingered on, whilst use of the type at Grays on route 375 ceased in May 1959. The final death-throes of T operation at Crawley in the 1960/61 period was to eventually attract some considerable and belated interest from enthusiasts.

Over on the north side, the last two in passenger use at Tring were withdrawn from use on routes 352 and 387 in May 1962. South of the Thames, a solitary survivor

hung on a little longer at Crawley for works services and occasional use on route 434 until August. The type then saw some very limited continued use as staff buses at various garages until sold, just one example still remaining for these duties by the end of 1962.

Disposals

What happened to the members of these four batches of buses after they fell from favour? The rundown of the 14T12 class was relatively steep, whereas the two variants of TD and the 15T13s took rather longer to disappear. The entire batch of 14T12s lasted until 1955, with all going by 1958. In contrast, the TD types took from 1956 until 1962 to disappear, with the 15T13s taking from 1957 until 1962.

The pattern of disposals naturally followed the pattern of withdrawals, but with some delays as buses awaited sale by tender, or in the case of some of the Country Area Regal IIIs, further use as staff buses.

The first buses of the four variants to go, the 14T12s, were still very much in early middle age, and so readily found new purchasers. The first eight went to a London dealer, the ominously-titled BSE, in summer 1955, with 13 more following in 1956. Most of the total batch of 50 – at least 28, though more may finally have been involved – went to the Ceylon (now Sri Lanka) Transport Board, which doubtless was well-pleased with its fine acquisitions, frowning or otherwise.

No details are to hand of any other UK purchasers of 14T12s, other than the sale of T745 to London SW18 scrap merchant Lammas Motors in early 1957, following a road traffic accident when in service. Any further information from readers, perhaps via Classic Bus, would be welcomed.

When the Weymann 1TD1 type came on the market, it was still a nearly-new design of bus. But many examples were fated in the event to see less than a

Was there ever a more handsome-looking single-decker than the 15T13 design? Here, T779 works Hemel Hempstead's duty 29 on route 377A on 28 June 1952. It is wearing the later simplified livery of Lincoln green with a narrow 'Chiswick Cream' relief band.

decade of service. In a UK context, it was already chronically outdated. By the late 1950s, Britain was already approaching the era of the Atlantean and the Routemaster, whilst the single-deck market was increasingly dominated by much more modern-looking stock such as the Leyland Tiger Cub. The coach market had undergone a similar Chinese-style 'great leap forward' from models such as the dependable Bedford OB to the underfloor-engine layout. Halfcab single-deckers were already obsolete by the mid-1950s.

However, there was still a demand from distant markets where operating staff labour was cheap and plentiful. The Weymann TD was therefore to find ready buyers in Yugoslavia, to where five (TD1/3-5/7) were exported in 1956 after sale via Milburn Motors to Birds of Stratford, and in Ceylon (Sri Lanka), where almost the entire remainder of the batch of 31 were exported to during the years 1958-60.

In actual fact, Milburn Motors bought seven buses, and so it remains a mystery as to quite what happened to TD2 and TD6. The likelihood is that they went either to Yugoslavia or Ceylon.

Indeed, Ceylon was to prove a hungry market, not only for the 14T12s and 1TD1s, as already noted, but also for the 1/1TD1s and the 15T13 Regals. In 1958, for instance, no fewer than 39 buses of all four types were shipped eastwards during the year. Interestingly, buses were exported not only carrying full LT livery but complete with fleetnames and numbers, though they were re-registered with their new owners.

The disposal of the 100 1/1TD1 buses was more complicated than that of the 31 earlier TDs, and it was very fortunate that this was the case, or there would be no TDs at all in preservation today.

TDs 32-53/5-7/5-8/8/91-94/6-8/102/7-11/3/5/7/9/20/2/5/7, a total of 74, went to the Ceylon Transport Board. The remainder were sold to dealers

and other purchasers in the UK.

Of these latter, TD54 went to a London SW17 contractor as staff transport, whilst TD99 and TD112 went to another contractor or industrial concern, Leach of Hayes. TD100/4/5 went to yet another London contractor, Sullivan of London SE15, and TD101 went to a further contractor, Wyatt of London E16. Meanwhile, TD74/90/106/123/131 passed to Birds, and at least three, TD74/90/106, went to a contractor in South Wales. Their ultimate fate is unknown, nor are details of the further careers of TD123/131 to hand. Birds were breakers as well as dealers, so any unsold stock might well have eventually found a new buyer in fragment form.

TD86/103/124 unusually went to the WRVS, and their ultimate fate, too, is not known. TD87 went to the Mayflower Family Centre in Canning Town, with disposal not recorded, but TD89 passed by the same way into eventual preservation. TD95 appears to have gone straight into preservation, still a fairly unusual move in those hard-up days of early appeals and rescues. TD114 went to BSP Industries of Borehamwood, presumably as a works bus.

TD118, following withdrawal after the last day at Kingston, went to Tillotson of London NW6. This latter bus was presumably the grey(?) caravan that I used to see parked nose-against-the-wall on the east side of Finchley Central station yard around 1969. It reputedly travelled as far as Greece and Turkey.

TD126 seems also to have been sold for contractors' use, as does TD129. Finally, TD130 appears to have also seen some unspecified contractor use before preservation. As can be seen, there are still some loose ends to the above, and so any further details, via CB, would be welcomed.

As noted already, the 15T13 Regals had begun to be sold off from 1956. Unfortunately for enthusiasts, once

T790 awaits departure on 22 July 1952 on Garston garage's duty 58, working the 309 to Rickmansworth Station (Met).

again no fewer than 21 of the 30 went to the Ceylon Transport Board, between 1958 and 1960, and are presumed to have either long since been scrapped or to have rapidly rotted away.

Of the remaining nine, T780/1 went to Shell in 1958 as staff transport. Dealer Vass of Ampthill, Bedfordshire, took a number, including T785/90/2, these later passing to the contractor Bovis in 1963. A Mansfield contractor purchased T787, the very last to be sold by LT, in summer 1963. The final fate of T772/4/6 is not to hand. Perhaps in a forgotten barn, somewhere . . .

Preservation

With their relatively early demise, four decades or more ago, these four sub-classes of single-decker might have been expected to become extinct. Interestingly, too, none of any type was set aside for official preservation by London Transport, perhaps due to their off-the-peg nature. The failure to officially preserve a postwar TD or T now looks a little surprising.

As the 14T12 class has completely disappeared, and as the surviving TD Tigers are of the later Mann Egerton species, the Weymann bodywork from both AEC and Leyland batches is wholly unrepresented in London bus preservation. However, the LT bus preservationist is a particularly determined species, and, as already hinted at, no fewer than four of the TD type, plus one of the handsome 15T13 vehicles, has survived into the 21st century.

The position with the Mann Egerton 1/TD2 batch is by far the brightest of the four types under review, remarkably so since the T and TD disappeared from London service when privately-promoted bus preservation was very much in its infancy and when

finding £80 to rescue a bus was way beyond the means of most enthusiasts.

In fact, five buses initially went into preservation, these being TD89, TD95, TD118, TD121 and TD130, though only four now remain and reunions are very rare events. Indeed, it is very doubtful if the four have ever been reunited in preservation.

TD89 passed to the TD89 Group in Surrey, and is now with Timebus, where a total rebuilding is approaching completion. Also, as is well known, TD95 became part of the London Bus Preservation Group (now Trust) fleet, eventually taking up residence at Cobham Bus Museum. Major reconstruction of the bodywork has taken place, and the bus is now in generally excellent condition, with a secure future.

After its spell as a caravan, TD118 passed rapidly through the hands of several preservationists, presumably being resold as each one assessed the major task of complete timber framing renewal and then thought better of it. It is now with preservationist Dick Bole, though it has yet to make an appearance fully restored. TD121 is the one out of the quintet that got away, being initially preserved but later vandalised and then sadly dismantled for spares. Given the development of enthusiast skills in recent years, this decision now seems extremely regrettable.

TD 130 had operated from eight London Transport garages when it was finally withdrawn in 1962. In 1964, the bus passed to Hills (Patents) Ltd of Staines, who repainted it into its blue livery. It passed into preservation in 1966, changing hands a number of times until ending up stored in a Sussex barn in the 1980s. In 1991 it was purchased by well-known Cobham Bus Museum member Roy Adams, though it is garaged elsewhere. It is also believed that at least

T791 is seen here in 1948 at Uxbridge station, when new, in the initial and very attractive livery of Lincoln green with broken white relief. The garage code WT16 behind the cab door refers to the small Watford Leavesden Road garage, which was later replaced by Garston.

one TD, possibly more, may still exist in Sri Lanka, converted to a lorry.

Lastly, we turn to the continued preservation of an example of the attractive 15T13 type. AEC Regal T792 was preserved by the late Alan Allmey, then by Don Allmey and most recently by John Herting. The bus had been one of Leavesden Road's batch when new in 1948, and had survived to become one of the last four in service when withdrawn in 1963. It had then, as noted, worked as contractors' transport with Bovis at Bedford between 1963 and 1966, before being rescued for preservation. Some readers may recall a colour illustration of sister vehicle T762, in Bovis grey livery, outside Aldershot Station in March 1965, published in David Kaye's long out of print pocketbook, 'Buses and Trolleybuses Since 1945'.

Interestingly, T792 now has an RT engine, the original worn unit being replaced in 1988. The conversion also involved changing the water pump and making modifications to the oil filler and dynamo, but has ensured that this unique bus can now be maintained in running order for decades to come.

Finally, although the London 14T12 type is extinct, it is well worth mentioning that a couple of near-identical complete examples from Devon General and an example from the Hebble fleet that was cut-down to a towing vehicle, very fortunately still exist to remind us of how handsome and workmanlike this design was. A good illustration of a Hebble example in ex-works condition appears in 'The Best of British Buses – AEC Regals', by Alan Townsin.

Retrospective

The postwar T and TD era had undoubtedly been a relatively short one, particularly when compared with the subsequent longevity of the RF, RT and RM.

Nevertheless, it had still spanned 16 years at its maximum, from 1946 until 1962, which is quite a presentable record when compared with many other types outside London, and even more so when set against the lifespan of some later off-the-peg designs within the Capital.

Several factors had worked to cut short the T and TD era. Firstly, at just 211 buses in total, there were not that many of them by LT's standards. Indeed, if one adds the 700 RF total to the 84 GS total and the 211 T/TD total, the last-mentioned in combination make up only just over one-fifth of the grand total of 995 single-deck vehicles delivered between 1946 and 1954. With the GS type specifically needed for its dwindling specialist role, and the RF dominating everything else, the Ts and TDs never really stood a chance. Indeed, one suspects that with hindsight, after the 1958 bus strike, a more determined effort might have seen them meet their end even earlier.

The growing availability of surplus RF vehicles (more could probably have been squeezed out if a tighter ship had been run by LT), and the conversion of some routes to RLH or RT family double-deck operation, also told against the Regals and Tigers.

Had Hitler not so brutally intervened, London Transport might also have been able to both sustain its existing 1930s single-deck fleet for a little longer, and to commence its quest for an underfloor-engined design a little earlier, with deliveries of the latter in place by, say, 1949-51 instead of 1951-53. These combined measures would have rendered the Ts and TDs unnecessary from the outset, and enabled the entire Regal and Tiger phase to have been missed out altogether. But London bus enthusiasts would all have been just a little the poorer for that. **CB**

A BLAST FROM THE PAST

GAVIN BOOTH dusts off some Box Brownie photos from his teenage years

Left: Technically not a great picture, but with a Box Brownie you had no control over anything. One of Midland Red's all-Leyland PD2s, class LD8, somewhere in leafy Warwickshire in 1959, when the Booth family was holidaying in Leamington Spa. Just imagine that shot in colour . . .

All photos by Gavin Booth

Below: On that same holiday, a trip to Coventry produced this photo of corporation no.78, a Daimler CVA6 with Metro-Cammell bodywork, one of a batch of 96 delivered in 1948-50. I probably took the photo because no.78 was not unlike Edinburgh Corporation's 72 Birmingham-style Daimlers.

Above: **Norfolk was another popular destination for family holidays and on a day trip to Great Yarmouth I caught this 1959 Albion Nimbus with 31-seat Willowbrook body, one of six.**

Left: **The Booth family was dragged to Surrey Docks for this photo of London Transport Routemaster RM1 – pity I misjudged the positioning in the fairly basic viewfinder.**

Above: **Now preserved, McGill, Barrhead GVD 47, the Red & White-style Guy Arab III with Duple 57-seat body, dating from 1950. It is laying over in the middle of the road in St James Street, Paisley – something you certainly couldn't do 40-odd years later.**

Below: **Low bridges between Falkirk and Edinburgh meant that Alexander (Midland) double-deckers were rarely seen in Edinburgh. This Stirling-based one did make it, though; it is MRC4 from a unique batch of AEC Regent III with this attractive style of Alexander 53-seat lowbridge bodywork, supplied in 1951. They were always out of place in a fleet dominated by Leyland, and later Bristol, double-deckers and it was surprising they did not find their way into the AEC-dominated Scottish Omnibuses fleet.**

Above: Whitesands, Dumfries has long been the terminus for longer-distance services to the town, and here in 1960 is L177, a 1940 Leyland Tiger TS8 with 1951 Alexander 39-seat body. On the right are D306, a 1946 AEC Regal with 1955 Bristol 53-seat lowbridge body, and D331, a 1947 AEC Regent with Northern Counties 53-seat lowbridge body.

Below: In the closing days of 1961 I managed to breach the normally impenetrable fortress that was Edinburgh Corporation's Shrubhill Works, to find no.604, the first of a batch of 50 Leyland Titan PD2A/30 with 66-seat Alexander bodies, newly arrived from Falkirk. On the left is another chassis from the batch, receiving Edinburgh's favoured BMMO-style front in place of the St Helens front fitted by Leyland. Also on the left is a Commer Cob patrol van.

MILESTONES IN DOUBLE-DECK BUS DESIGN

GAVIN BOOTH looks at the bus that set the trend for half-a-century

Leyland Atlantean

Was there life before the Atlantean?

There was, of course. For 50 years since the early years of the 20th century the double-deck bus had been going through a process of steady evolution. The London Transport Routemaster, although it wasn't the last of the front-engined double-deckers to be developed, probably represented the ultimate manifestation of that genre, but engineers were already looking at alternative layouts.

Rear-engined buses were not new; they could be found in various parts of the world, but they were rare in Britain. In 1939 Leyland had developed a rear-engined version of its Cub chassis for London Transport and in 1950 Foden had introduced a rear-engined coach, but on double-deckers the engine looked set to stay at the front.

Leyland had other ideas and in 1952 showed an experimental rear-engined bus, the Lowloader, which was used to test the water. The chassis layout was unusual, and very different from the rear-engined buses that would come later. The engine was mounted on the rear platform, and the driver sat over the front

axle. Leyland used a turbocharged version of its O.350 engine, coupled to a preselective gearbox, and in this form the first prototype was tried by operators throughout the country; at the same time, Leyland was rethinking the whole concept.

When the Atlantean was launched in 1956 it was a very different animal. But even this was not the final answer. Until 1956 two-axle double-deckers were restricted to a 27ft (8.2m) length, and the maximum seating total was 66. Now Leyland could offer a real crowd-mover, and the Atlantean offered 78 seats. The engine was now the O.600, familiar to Titan operators, and the entrance was ahead of the front axle, under the control of the driver. In outline it was to define the shape of British double-deckers for years to come. Under the skin it was a semi-integral bus with bodywork by Metro-Cammell, Leyland's partner on the Olympic series of single-deckers, and it achieved a commendably low overall height of 13ft 3in (4.03m).

Operator feedback may have caused Leyland to rethink how it offered the Atlantean. While low height was important to some operators, it was not an issue in most urban fleets. What may have been more of an issue was the integral construction. British operators liked the chassis-and-body concept, particularly when it allowed them to choose their own favoured

The 1956 prototype integral Atlantean, 281 ATC, at the Metro-Cammell coachworks just after completion. It is easy to see how the appearance of this bus caused a sensation.

bodybuilders and body designs. So the Atlantean was redesigned as a chassis.

So, what was different about the Atlantean?

At first glance, just about everything, but for the more conservative busmen there were familiar elements like the trusted Leyland O.600 engine and Pneumocyclic gearbox, though these were mounted at exactly the opposite end of the bus, which was something bus operators would have to get used to. For many the attraction was the increased seating capacity this layout could offer – up to 78 – at a time when the use of fewer bigger buses was seen as one way of counteracting increasing costs and reducing passenger numbers.

Leyland's sensible decision to reinvent the Atlantean as a chassis with familiar 'big bus' components meant that the model lost its inbuilt lowheight advantage, but recognised that there was still a market for buses that were lower than the normal height of around 14ft 6in (4.41m). With a fairly high-frame chassis the only way to achieve this was with a rather unwieldy upper deck arrangement; this was normal towards the front, but to retain normal headroom on the lower deck over the rear axle some height had to be taken from the upper deck, resulting in a few rows of lowbridge-style four-across seats and a side gangway. The result was 13ft 4in (4.06m) high.

Where Leyland went did others follow?

Yes, but not right away. The arrival of the Atlantean coincided with the relaxation to 30ft double-deckers and so some bus companies got their extra seats in more conventional ways – by buying longer versions of the buses they already operated. So long AEC Regents, Bristol Lodekkas, Daimler CVGs, Guy Arabs and Leyland Titans were ordered, many with entrances mounted just behind the rear axle; but right up to the end of front-engined double-deckers at the end of the 1960s there were extremely traditional buses being bought, with exposed radiators and rear entrances – direct descendants of those 1927 Titan TD1s.

Leyland's rivals were obviously watching the Atlantean with interest. In 1956 AEC had introduced the Bridgemaster, a front-engined lowheight integral double-decker and persevered with its Regent and later Renown front-engined models. AEC merged with Leyland in 1962 and this inevitably affected just what new models would be produced. AEC worked with London Transport on a rear-engined Routemaster, which appeared in 1966, and although there had been plans to sell this commercially, they never came to fruition.

Guy went in a different direction with its Wulfrunian, still with a front-mounted engine but with the entrance ahead of the front axle. The Wulfrunian was a brave try – foolhardy, some might say – but Guy was in trouble, and the Wulfrunian probably added to its woes.

Bristol kept going with its Lodekka for its Tilling and Scottish group customers, but with 1965 changes that brought Bristol into a closer relationship with Leyland and back into the open market, it developed its VR chassis, first as the VRL with longitudinal rear engine, and then as the VRT, with transverse rear engine, like the others.

The one company that gave Leyland's Atlantean a really good run for its money was Daimler, which in 1960 introduced its Fleetline. For many operators the Fleetline had two advantages over the Atlantean: it was designed from scratch as a lowheight model and came with the Gardner 6LX engine, a unit revered by generations of engineers. With the Fleetline there was no need for that ungainly upper deck layout and for operators needing lowheight buses the Fleetline was usually the model of choice. Leyland responded with Atlantean variations in the Fleetline mould, but with limited success.

For the 1960s and 1970s the Atlantean and Fleetline were the main double-deck choices in Britain, and although other model came in and nibbled at the edges, they didn't really get a look in. Leyland kept the Atlantean on the model lists until 1984, but by that time it was looking a bit tired, in spite of what was essentially a relaunch in 1972 with the AN68 series. Leyland's big plan – and this was during its Leyland-knows-best phase – was to replace the Atlantean, Fleetline and VRT with one all-singing model, the Titan, which had been designed with more than half an eye on London business, and which Leyland decided would be acceptable everywhere else. Bus operators were decidedly unconvinced, and the outcome was a Bristol-developed model, the Olympian, which would go on to be a worthy successor to the Atlantean. **CB**

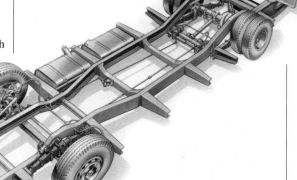

ROGER AND OUT

To ROGER DAVIES goes the last word, this time on the vexed question of registration marks. Oh yes, and trim. And moustaches and brothels . . .

I WATCHED AN EDITION OF 'DOCTOR WHO'. It was set in London, many of the shots were obviously filmed there. But as the good doctor now resides in Cardiff, clearly some shots were done in that city for, as some London suburb was being sought, a Cardiff Bus Dennis Dart passed quietly behind. Later a big red bus was provided, but with too much white for Ken's liking and I'm pretty sure it was an East Lancs demonstrator. Some years ago, an excellent TV programme, 'Our friends in the North' was slightly marred for me as 1970s Newcastle played host to a Stagecoach double deck.

So what is this all about and where is it leading? Don't worry, for I have only the vaguest clue, so, Doctor Who-like, let's see where the ride takes us.

Recognition, that's what it's all about. A big part of our hobby in days gone by was the ability to identify an operator's buses by significant features. In these days of heavily-standardised types, it is almost impossible and a home-grown product looks just the same as one that may have had quite a thrilling existence.

A great clue was the registration number. That's what it was called, a number. The current system has a few numbers, totally worthless (is it an 06 56 or an 07 56?) and it is completely unmemorable. Added to which it tells you precious little about the origins of the vehicle and, to be quite honest, I don't see why the enthusiast press bothers with recording them. (Incidentally, it was claimed the Police liked the scheme but I've since heard they weren't even asked.)

So, if it was EO it was a Barrow bus (even if it had been sold to Merthyr Tydfil, who were, of course HB) and TP would be Portsmouth. You had to be careful though, CK and RN were Ribble but just could be Preston Corporation, a sneaky trick for the unwary. Similarly, CD or UF were Southdown but could be Brighton Corporation (but never Brighton Hove & District). Midland Red was HA and no one else was. Typical. This was a great help in tracking down buses with subsequent owners. Luckily it was far less common for municipal buses to see further service, unlike company ones, particularly Ribble and Southdown ones. Midland Reds rarely did, so Hah! Or should that be Ha?

Top: **JEO 769**, so it must be a Barrow Corporation bus, and indeed it is. Seen in its hometown in January 1976, no.69 is an East Lancs-bodied Leyland Leopard with 42 seats and two doors, dating from 1963. One of a batch of six, the first of this combination, this type soon, with longer and more modern, but I would say not so attractive bodywork, became Barrow's standard bus ousting what had, in its turn, been a pretty standardised fleet of Park Royal bodied PD2s.

All photos by Roger Davies

Left: Typical of later Barrow PD2 Park Royals was this most agreeable-looking bus. However the registration, **HB 8799**, gives it away as a Merthyr Tydfil Corporation bus. Curiously, this fleet too moved from a Titan-based fleet (although with various body styles and lengths) on to East Lancs-bodied Leopards and the kit surrounding no.84 in the bus station in August 1969 would have been equally at home in Barrow. That strange rear window always reminded me of a garden shed for some reason. The link between these two far-removed fleets was even stronger, Merthyr having bought 10 PD2s from Barrow in 1961. All added to the interest.

And when you are presented with this, the registration is all you've got going for you! This is at Arlington sales depot in Penarth Road Cardiff (now vanished under flyovers, flyunders, superstores and the usual faceless 21st century stuff) and it is in the livery of a subsequent owner, R I Davies of Tredegar. There in May 1967 was this amazing beast, an Atkinson BPM746H with Weymann 42-seat rear entrance body dating from 1952. How do I know all this? Well the FDB 504 registration led me to North Western. It may have been Stockport Corporation but that was unlikely! Atkinsons were never common, this one was part of a batch of 12 numbered 500 to 511. Staggeringly, nearby Lancashire United took a batch of Atkinsons numbered 490 to 499 a year later! Look how R I Davies has adjusted his grey and red livery to the body trim.

This in turn led on to all sorts of things. Birmingham City Transport had all 999 numbers in the JOJ series and Glasgow and, of all people, Western National attempted similar tricks with FYS and SGD in the former's case and LTA in the latter's. Why? It meant buses entering service with registrations way out of date. But it was memorable, different, interesting. The British Bus Fleets book including Western National (no.8) even had a breakdown of the LTA series.

Routemasters

Oh dear, so now we need to move on to London Transport and, worse still Routemasters. But, and this is a nice thing, the first batches had LT registrations, SLT, VLT, WLT, and reversed CLT. (OK, so RM1000 was 100 BXL; did they miss BLT or did they have a portent of the rather odd sandwich concoction that is now so common? I like my BLT without L and T thanks). They then lurched off into DYE; I don't think DJ Dave Lee Travis, alias DLT, was that well-known then, so it is a bit of a sad regression. (Incidentally, talking of LT – why did they re-register the RT in Cliff Richard's movie 'Summer Holiday'? Looks like a brand-new registration to me. But what do I know? See, an added enjoyment to the movie – perhaps the only enjoyment?)

Anyway, maybe there was some move of registration office. Moves could have an effect. The sensational Neath & Cardiff Luxury Coaches moved their Head Office from Swansea to Briton Ferry and then had to register their coaches in the County of Glamorgan rather than Swansea. And registering in counties rather than towns meant you could be really baffled as to the origins of a bus. Lancashire and said Glamorgan could boast innumerable companies on their books and tracing a bus you didn't know could be quite a task.

I'm not saying the old system had any logic to it, but it was just so interesting and added to the enjoyment of buses. Just dwell a moment on this. A bus with UA or UB would be Leeds City Transport, UC would be a London bus, UD a South Midland one, UE a Stratford Blue, UF Southdown (or Brighton), UG back to Leeds, UH Cardiff or Western Welsh, UJ somewhere to lead us to UK in Wolverhampton. What about that then! UM was Leeds too, but, as rather politely put by Buses Illustrated magazine, the 'B' multiples were not used.

Then you had personal intervention. Charles Baroth, the charismatic general manager of Salford City Transport, insisted all Salford's buses be in the RJ series. I know not why, but I think it must have been right because under Mr Baroth's leadership, Salford City Transport was one of the, if not the finest bus fleet in the UK. OK so I'm biased, the livery was green, but what presentation, the buses were magnificent! Pity about the operating area . . .

And then came 1974 and a huge amalgamation of licensing offices. Suddenly, buses could appear with registrations from far afield, Cardiff Bus had some VRTs registered like Red & White buses based in Chepstow! Outrageous. And, at first, many licensing authorities refused to allocate requested numbers, so, after a long time where most people had matched fleet and registration numbers, this became impossible. For a company like East Kent, where the registration was

Left: Western National had all of LTA 723 to 999 but the buses carrying these registrations were delivered over a five-year period, 1949 to 1953, during which time buses with other registration letters entered service. Goodness knows why. LTA 993 here, a Bristol KSW6B, was delivered in 1952 as no.1850 and, yes I know, was a Southern National bus. Buses with earlier numbers were delivered later, and indeed, new owner here, Smith's Coaches, also had LTA 987 a one-year newer LS5G formerly no.1690! I know all this because of the registration number. It is in Cardiff in September 1971 about to work the infrequent back roads route to St Brides between Cardiff and Newport.

Below: When based in Swansea, Neath & Cardiff coaches were registered there, but their move out of the town to Briton Ferry meant that coaches from 1965 onwards had Glamorganshire letters. The fleet included a rare and distinctive combination, 12 Guy Arab LUF coaches with Park Royal bodywork delivered in two batches over 1954 and 1955 which became synonymous with the fleet. One of the 1954 ones, KCY 489, nominally fleetnumber 34, is in Cardiff in April 1966. The 1955 batch had different body mouldings and the livery was amended accordingly. What a brute eh!

the fleetnumber, huge doses of paracetamol were the order of the day. Not all authorities were so bloody-minded and some operators took to registering their buses where they were built. And, horrors of all horrors, an 'S' multiple, always Scottish, WS, was allocated to... Bristol! I ask you; bureaucrats have no idea at all. The rot had set in, a key part of our hobby was going and, coupled with faceless PTEs with head offices in unlikely places, things didn't look good. At least the National Bus Company, despite corporate identity, still allowed local companies to take care of registering their buses.

If it's UE, its Stratford Blue, but none of these is playing ball! This delightful fleet had huge amounts of interest despite a fleet size of only 44. This view at their Warwick Road, Stratford depot in November 1966 demonstrates some of that with the two fairly standard BET single-deck Tiger Cubs, Marshall-bodied no.51 and Willowbrook-bodied no.42 standing out by their unusual registrations of 5451 WD and 2743 AC. For a small fleet it had a high proportion of reversed two-letter registrations. Pride of place goes to absolutely immaculate PD2 Leyland no.24, by now 14 years old! Bless them, Cardiff education department used to send us there regularly to see Shakespeare plays, this was the stunning 'Macbeth' starring David Warner fresh from his success as 'Morgan, a suitable case for treatment' in the movie of the same name. Magic, all this and no.24 too!

Dearneways had a noticeable presence in Sheffield, their dark blue buses adding interest. They went on a spending spree in South Wales buying a goodly number of apparently identical Weymann-bodied Tiger Cubs. One, however, NTG 141, was clearly an ex-Rhondda Glamorgan-registered bus whilst the others, including Cardiff-registered HUH 3 here were from the mighty group of 180 such buses built up by Western Welsh between 1953 and 1957. Formerly no.1003, this was the third one. Being passed by Sheffield AEC Regent V no.460, the bus is in Exchange Street, now much changed by Supertram.

Pitfalls

This was not without its pitfalls. On a visit to Eastern Coach Works in 1974, I noticed a large batch of Bristol LHs for Hants & Dorset with strange registrations and queried it with our guide. He coloured and said quietly 'Well 'J' sounds like 'A' over the phone.' Then there were buses that were diverted after registration. We did that with two VRTs at M&D, KKK 887/8V, which went to Alder Valley. I was concerned to read about one of these recently when it was referred to as ex-M&D. Although it was delivered to us and painted green it never turned a wheel for M&D so the claim was wrong. Funny how diversions tended to send red buses to green companies and vice versa. I had a red Olympian at M&D (diverted from Devon General in 1984 as being too big) and was prevented from painting it green as it had a demonstration type of paint! An overall advert soon sorted that!

This of course, was as nothing compared with the pre-corporate identity days when all sorts of interesting things happened. I still recall my shock at seeing a Willowbrook-bodied Atlantean in full Devon General

livery entering service with Yorkshire Traction. They had had time to reregister them, (747-750, RHE 447-450G) and as they worked on route 66, one I frequently used, they became firm friends. (It went from Sheffield where I was in college, to Bradford where Auntie lived. Family ties? Er, no – clothes washing and ironing actually.)

Then there were swaps of recently-delivered buses to what were deemed more deserving cases, which made it an interesting time. All South Wales Transport's AEC Swifts going to London Country springs to mind including diversions of some not yet delivered (the very fine Alexander-bodied SMAs). This never seemed very fair on SWT who entered a decidedly dicey period at the time (I remember seeing a pretty ex-Western Welsh Reliance in my time at WW in 1973 that was so filthy we wouldn't let it go back to Swansea) but you have to feel for LCBS inheriting 484 RTs. Someone was cute there and it wasn't NBC!

Talking of Western Welsh, in 1971 they were due 10 Alexander-bodied Atlanteans. The first five arrived, duly got registered VUH 377-381J and entered service.

The only clue here is the registration, TCP 900. Now it could be Halifax Corporation, but even for them, this unusual but very attractive Alexander-bodied Reliance is a bit out of the ordinary. So it can only be Hebble, a strange, quirky and rather likeable little BET company that carved itself out a living between Halifax and Leeds. By the time it was ambling through Matlock in June 1974, former no.74, dating from 1964, had passed to Silver Services of Darley Dale.

Now by this time, in response to car salesmen, or so it was alleged, the year-suffix letter, having been really sensible for the first four years (1963-66), had altered to change on August the first. It was claimed this avoided a surge on January the first, so it happened on August the first instead. And if it was to do with Christmas, why not a dispensation from December the 25th allowing use of next year's registration?

Red to blue

It was clearly bonkers and only a bureaucrat could come up with such rubbish. Anyway, back to the Atlanteans. The next five were due to enter service in August so, with another delightful twist of the old system, became registered VUH 382-386K! Except they didn't. They were diverted to East Yorkshire (red to blue in that case!) and got reregistered in Hull. One plate, VUH 385K graced a workbench in Western Welsh's main works for many years after. Just to finish the tale, the original five soon went to Western National (not only green but a firm Bristol user so some lunacy is apparent here) keeping their Cardiff registrations. Now you can't in all honesty say ten Alexander-bodied Atlanteans of the time were in any way exceptional, but with their registrations they make for an interesting tale.

Actually, the variety of colours helps too, it's rather like the London RLHs, many of which spent their whole time in the Capital painted green, then went to Samuel Ledgard of Leeds to become blue, ending up being exported to the USA and being painted red as are all London buses. Of course.

Which neatly brings us to trim. Often this was individually styled to match a fleet livery and became pretty ludicrous to look at if the livery was changed or adjusted. Perhaps the most classic was the beading around a band of colour that looked plain daft if that colour band was removed. But some were just plain quirky and for this we need to return to the splendid Maidstone & District company. Way before my time (although we did reintroduce it on our long-lived short Leopards), the company introduced a distinctive 'moustache' on the front panels of its buses which was painted cream on the otherwise green panel (actually, Mexborough & Swinton buses had this feature too). Buses retaining this feature could thus be easily identified as ex-M&D in a subsequent life. It is such a

one that leads us on to the next, and most exciting part of our tale.

One day I was contemplating not a lot really when the phone rang. It was a reporter from the local Chatham paper who had a question. I, after an early bad experience with the *Newcastle Journal* which has turned me against that publication ever since, always believed in fostering a good relationship with the press. Well, papers and radio, the jumped-up, self-important berks at TV can take a funny run. So I took the call. 'Have you sold an old double-decker bus to someone in Paris? A quick check with that fount of all knowledge, the M&D and East Kent Bus Club, elicited the necessary information and I was soon ringing back with the news that an Atlantean had indeed been sold to a group caring for underprivileged women in the French Capital. My contact reported that he had read about it in a column in a motoring magazine he favoured and the writer had spotted the bus and identified it as ex-M&D by the 'distinctive front moustache' on the bus. 'And him not even a bus spotter. I'd like to run a story', he said, 'thing is, it has changed a bit; it is now a mobile brothel.'

If it has an 'S' in it, it must be Scottish ... that is until the beastly bureaucrats got their hands on the system and transferred 'WS' to Bristol. Anyway, a reminder of happier times and this fabulous 1965 Duple Alpine Continental-bodied AEC Reliance, BSD 559C, one of two, is certainly Scottish belonging to the Dodd's of Troon fleet. That's Dodd's Coaches, not the buses which were part of the AA group and were always kept separate. When new, these two were painted two shades of grey for operation in Ireland for Global Tours. By this July 1976 view in Troon, the coach had gained the more attractive green and cream fleet livery.

So, we had some fun along the lines 'Its morals have slipped since it was with us', 'the only red lights on it here were stop lights', 'puts a new meaning on pay-as-you-enter and room for one more on top', and a delightful piece duly appeared. For some reason the reporter thought it very funny that the bus number was 5569. Can't think why.

Some weeks later, my father phoned to say I was in the *News of the World*, not a particular career aim, I have to say. Turns out the Chatham paper had syndicated the story and the *News of the World* had

Can we have two N&C pictures? Of course we can! The relatively large group of Guy Arabs took some replacing so secondhand purchases were undertaken. Never mind the distinctly Sheffield registration, the trim on the bodywork means that this coach could only have come from one fleet: Sheffield United Tours. It doesn't fit too easily with N&C livery but 3281 WB, formerly SUT no.281 of 1958 is a good match for what had become a predominately AEC fleet. It is at the N&C stop in Cardiff bus station, a local landmark meeting place, in January 1967 leading one of N&C's own coaches of the same type.

And so to trim. Absolutely fabulous Cardiff Corporation East Lancs-bodied AEC Regent V no.375 of 1961 shows the final version of the fully lined-out livery with black wings and edging to the cream bands. Next to it in this October 1965 view is one year newer no.385 where the cream has been reduced and the black gone altogether. This didn't make too much difference, but when the cream was reduced even further, these superb buses had strange marks, visible panty lines if you will, that meant nothing at all and detracted from their looks.

picked it up and even sent a photographer to Paris to picture the bus!

So there you go; something Mexborough & Swinton couldn't claim.

Probably.

Anyway, there it is, some other things lost to bus enthusiasm. In all honesty, they were not particularly good days for the bus industry and it most certainly didn't provide anything like the good service enjoyed in many places today. But I look back on those days, as an enthusiast, with great fondness and miss them.

Tried growing a moustache once. Looked silly. **CB**